STUDENT'S BOOK

Brainwa

LEVEL 3

OXFORD UNIVERSITY PRESS

Kate Wakeman • • • • • • • Danae Kozanoglou

Contents

Unit	Vocabulary *topic*	*lexical area*	Language focus	Skills focus

Vocabulary

1 c ___
2 c ___
3 c ___
4 e ___
5 d ___
6 k ___
7 t ___
8 b ___
9 t ___
10 s ___
11 b ___ w ___
12 g ___

1 🎞️ ① **Complete the labels. Then listen, repeat and check your answers.**

agle   hihuahua   lue   hale   amel

iraffe   iger   olphin   hark

ortoise   heetah   iwi   utterfly

2 Which group do the animals belong to?

a land animals   b sea animals   c birds   d insects

3 Describe the animals. Talk about what they look like and anything else you know about them.

4 Match the questions and answers.

☐ How long is it?
☐ How heavy is it?
☐ How tall is it?
☐ How fast can it run?

a

80 kilometres per hour

b
200,000 kilograms

c

3 metres

d

4 metres

5 Write the questions and answers to Exercise 3 in full.

How fast can a cheetah run?

It can run at 80 kilometres per hour.

6 Write more questions about any of the animals on this page.

Where do cheetahs live?

What do blue whales eat?

7 Do you know the answers to all of your questions in Exercise 6? If not, where can you look for them?

● Language focus

Do you know ...?

1 Cover Exercise 2. Do you know the answers to any of these questions?

1 <u>How many</u> bones are there in your body?

2 <u>How many</u> eggs can a mother crocodile lay?

3 <u>How far</u> can the North American bald eagle fly in a day?

4 <u>How long</u> does a mother elephant carry her baby in her body?

5 <u>How long</u> is a giraffe's tongue?

6 <u>How fast</u> can giraffes run?

7 <u>How many</u> kinds of butterflies are there in the world?

8 <u>How much</u> milk does a baby blue whale need every day?

2 Now read the answers and match them with the questions in Exercise 1.

a Over 300 km.

b About 15,000.

c Nearly 50 cm long.

d 600 litres.

e 206.

f 2 years.

g 65 kilometres per hour.

h 30.

Look!

How long ...? can mean two things.

| How long is your ruler? | 30 centimetres. |
| How long is this lesson? | 50 minutes. |

Questions

● Look at these three types of questions. Which type are all the questions in Exercise 1?

How ...? questions

How long is a crocodile?
It's 3 metres long.

How much does an elephant weigh?
It weighs 5 tonnes.

How many teeth has a kiwi got?
None.

Wh– questions

<u>What</u> do vampire bats drink?
Vampire bats drink <u>blood</u>.

<u>Which animal</u> drinks blood?
<u>The vampire bat</u> drinks blood.

<u>Where</u> do kiwis live?
They live in <u>New Zealand</u>.

Questions with *yes/no* answer

Can polar bears swim?   Yes, they can.

Do tigers live in Europe?   No, they don't.

Are polar bears bigger than tigers?
Yes, they are.

Have alligators got big teeth?
Yes, they have.

● As you do the other exercises in this unit, think about these different types of questions and find more examples.

3 Use question words to complete these questions.

1 ..... do polar bears live?

2 ..... legs has a spider got?

3 ..... snakes swim?

4 ..... animal sleeps upside down?

5 ..... a tiger bigger than a lion?

6 ..... dolphins a kind of fish?

7 ..... do blue whales eat?

8 ..... does a giant tortoise weigh?

4 Work in pairs. Try to find answers for the questions in Exercise 3. Where can you look?

5 Ask questions using *biggest, fastest, heaviest, smallest*, etc.

Which animal is the heaviest?
The blue whale.

Skills focus

The Brainwaves Quiz Show

1   Look at the picture. What is a quiz show?

ANIMALS

1 The cheetah
2 The chihuahua
3 The elephant
4 About 5,000 kg

PLACES

5 Istanbul
6 Brazil
7 In Giza, Egypt
8 In Athens, Greece

SPACE

9 The Milky Way
10 300,000 km per second
11 About 4,000,000,000 years
12 About 149,000,000 km

2   Read the answer cards. Can you think of possible questions?

3   ▭ ❷ Listen to the quizmaster. What do the teams have to do?

4   Try to complete the quizmaster's questions. Then match them to answers 1–12 on the cards.

  a ..... are the pyramids?   7
  b What is the ..... kind of dog?   ☐
  c ..... is the biggest land animal?   ☐
  d Which is the biggest ..... in Latin America?   ☐
  e ..... is the name of our galaxy?   ☐
  f Which is the biggest ..... in Turkey?   ☐
  g How ..... does light travel?   ☐
  h How ..... away is the Sun?   ☐
  i How ..... does an elephant weigh?   ☐
  j ..... is the Acropolis?   ☐
  k ..... old is the Earth?   ☐
  l What is the ..... animal on land?   ☐

5   ▭ ❸ Listen and check your answers to Exercise 4. Which team wins round one?

Speaking tip

When you ask questions, use appropriate intonation. To practise, listen and repeat the questions in Exercises 4 and 5.

6   Prepare round two of the quiz. In groups, write more questions and answers for each topic.

7   Play round two. Each group takes it in turns to choose a topic. They then have to answer another group's question on that topic. The winning group is the one which answers the most questions correctly.

Wonderful World

8 Look at the picture.

   a   How does the boy feel?

   b   Do you think he is a good student? Why? / Why not?

9 **Listen to the song. What does he say about these things?**

History   Biology   Science
French   Geography
Trigonometry   Algebra

10 **Make a list of things that you don't know much about. Use your list to change the words of the song. Then sing your own version!**

Think about it!

1   **Match the words and pictures.**

tortoise ☐   dolphin ☐   cheetah ☐   shark ☐

① ② ③ ④

2   **Write questions. The underlined words give the answers.**

1   Birds eat <u>butterflies</u>.
    What .... ?

2   That man weighs <u>75 kilos.</u>
    .... ?

3   Cape Town is <u>in South Africa</u>.
    .... ?

4   <u>900 people</u> live in the Vatican City.
    .... ?

5   Concorde can fly at <u>2,150 kilometres an hour</u>.
    .... ?

3   **Write short answers to the questions.**

1   Can alligators run fast?   ....

2   Do eagles eat meat?   ....

3   Have giraffes got short necks? ....

4   **Write questions and answers about your country.**

1   Which / long / river
    .... ?
    ....

2   Where / high / mountain
    .... ?
    ....

3   Which / big / city
    .... ?
    ....

Choose and circle.

Easy   OK   Difficult

UNIT 2 • What's in a dish?

● Vocabulary

beef   eggs   oil   spices   cheese
flour   onions   sugar   chicken
lettuce   potatoes   tomatoes   corn   milk
rice   tuna   cream   mushrooms

dairy products

1 e g g s

2 _ _ _ _ _

3 _ _ _ _

4 _ _ _ _ _ _

meat and fish

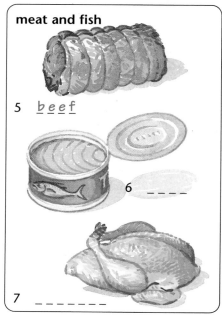

5 b e e f

6 _ _ _ _

7 _ _ _ _ _ _

fruit and vegetables

8 t o m a t o e s

9 _ _ _ _ _ _ _

10 _ _ _ _ _ _

11 _ _ _ _ _ _

12 _ _ _ _ _ _ _ _

grain

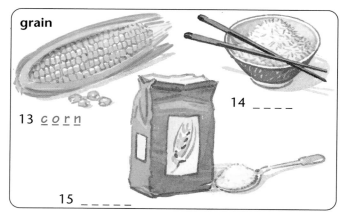

13 c o r n

14 _ _ _ _

15 _ _ _ _ _

other

16 o i l

17 _ _ _ _ _ _

18 _ _ _ _ _

---

1 **Match the words and pictures.**

2 ▭ ❶ **Listen and check your answers. Then listen and repeat.**

3 **Add more words to each of the five groups. Ask your teacher for words you need or use a dictionary.**
    dairy products: yoghurt, …

4 **What ingredients do you need to make these dishes?**

a cheese omelette   a hamburger   tuna salad

5 **Think of other dishes. Say what ingredients you need to make them.**

● Language focus

Home Economics

1 Read the introduction and look at the pictures. Answer these questions:

  a What is a Home Economics class?

  b What are the children doing?

This is my Home Economics class. Today, we're learning about dishes from different countries.

2 Read the list of ingredients and look at the ticks in column 1 of the table. What ingredients do you need to make spring rolls?

You need flour, …

Ingredients	1 spring rolls	2 curry	3 tacos	4 calzone
flour	✔			
corn				
meat	✔			
mushrooms	✔			
tomatoes				
vegetables	✔			
lettuce				
onions				
chillies				
garlic				
cheese				
spices				

3 ❷ Listen to dialogue 1 and answer the questions.

  a What are spring rolls made with?

  b What are they filled with?

  c What are they served with?

4 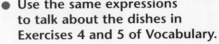 ❸ Listen to dialogues 2, 3 and 4 and complete the table in Exercise 2.

5 Listen to all four dialogues again and check your answers.

> **FOCUS**
>
> **made with …**
>
> - **Use these expressions to talk about curry, tacos and calzone.**
>   It's/They're made with …
>   It's/They're filled with …
>   It's/They're served with …
> - **Use the same expressions to talk about the dishes in Exercises 4 and 5 of Vocabulary.**

6 Now read and complete the dialogues.

Dialogue 1

Oliver   What are these?

Girl   They're spring rolls. They're made with ¹..... . They're filled with ²....., ³..... and ⁴..... . They're served with soy sauce or chilli sauce.

Dialogue 2

Oliver   What's this?

Boy   It's curry. It's made with ¹....., ²....., ³....., garlic, and lots of ⁴..... . It's served with rice. Be careful, it's hot – but very tasty!

Dialogue 3

Oliver   What are these?

Girl   They're tacos. Tacos are made with ¹..... . They're filled with ²....., tomatoes, ³....., ⁴..... and ⁵..... . Here – have some.

Dialogue 4

Oliver   What's this funny bread?

Boy   It's not bread, it's an Italian pizza. It's called calzone and it's made with ¹..... . It's filled with ²....., ³....., tomatoes, and ⁴..... . It's delicious! Don't touch it – I have to cook it first!

Oliver   Oh, sorry!

7 Role-play similar dialogues about other dishes.

● Skills focus

Mayonnaise monsters

1 Look at the photos. What do you think the teacher is doing?

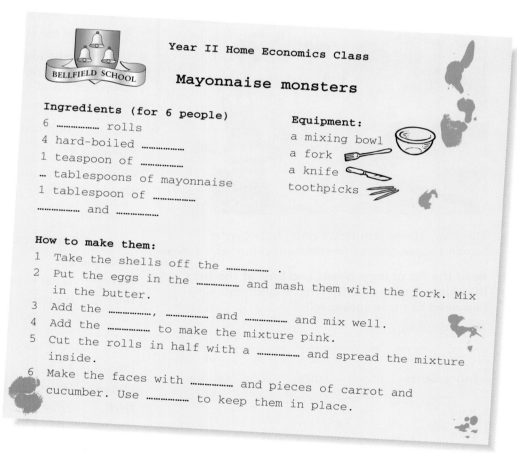

Year II Home Economics Class

Mayonnaise monsters

BELLFIELD SCHOOL

Ingredients (for 6 people)
6 .... rolls
4 hard-boiled ....
1 teaspoon of ....
... tablespoons of mayonnaise
1 tablespoon of ....
.... and ....

Equipment:
a mixing bowl
a fork
a knife
toothpicks

How to make them:
1 Take the shells off the ....
2 Put the eggs in the .... and mash them with the fork. Mix in the butter.
3 Add the ...., ... and .... and mix well.
4 Add the .... to make the mixture pink.
5 Cut the rolls in half with a .... and spread the mixture inside.
6 Make the faces with .... and pieces of carrot and cucumber. Use .... to keep them in place.

2 🎞️ ④ Listen to the first part of the recipe. Complete the list of ingredients.

3 Look at the list of equipment. Find the things in the photos.

4 🎞️ ⑤ Listen to the rest of the recipe. Number the pictures in the correct order.

5 Listen again. Write the missing words.

6 In groups, think of other kinds of sandwiches. Write a list of ingredients and a simple recipe.

Listening tip

When you have to listen for specific information, try to think of possible answers before you listen. Use pictures and the rest of the text to help you.

Food, glorious food!

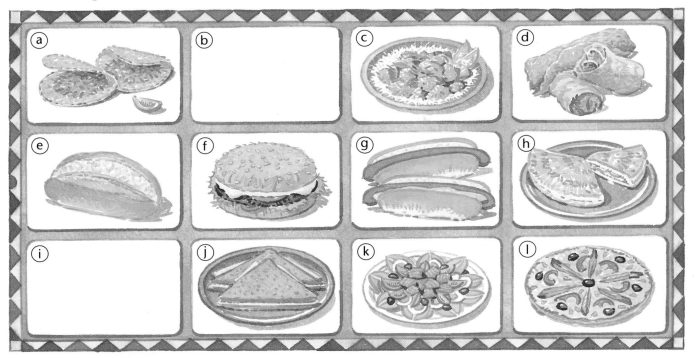

1 **Look at the pictures. Think about:**
   a what each dish is called
   b what each dish is made of

2 **Write dishes from your country in the two blank squares.**

3 **Write the letters a–l on 12 slips of paper. Put them face down on the desk.**

4 **Choose a slip of paper and find the right pictures.**

   a Say what the dish is called. Then say at least three more things about it:

   d! Those are spring rolls. They're from China. They're filled with vegetables and meat …

   b If someone chooses the same picture again, he or she has to talk about a dish from his or her country.

Think about it!

1 **Complete the instructions. Use each word from the list once.**

   | lettuce   garlic   bowl   pieces   tuna   ~~salad~~ |
   | fork   tomatoes   mayonnaise |

   Today we are going to make a ¹salad............ .
   First, you'll need a large ².................... to put it
   in. You'll also need a ³............. and a spoon to
   serve it with. Choose a large green
   ⁴............................ and cut it into small
   ⁵.......................... . Then cut up some red
   ⁶.......................... and onions. Mix in one
   tablespoonful of ⁷.......................... . Add a little
   ⁸.......................... but not too much! Finally,
   put some ⁹.......................... fish on the top.
   Serve it straight away.

2 **Answer the questions.**

   1 What are hamburgers made with?
      ....
   2 What are they usually served with?
      ....

3 **Describe your favourite sandwich.**
   It's made with ....
   and filled with ....

   Choose and circle.

   Easy   OK   Difficult

SCHOOL LIFE
PEOPLE AND PLACES
FREE TIME
ENTERTAINMENT

Vocabulary

☐	fly through the flames	☐	climb down the cliff	☐	jump into the plane
1	climb up the building	☐	jump over the train	☐	dive into the sea
☐	ride up the bridge	☐	fall off the motorcycle	☐	land on the motorcycle
☐	swim under water	☐	walk to the edge of the roof	☐	get on to the jetski
☐	jump out of the plane	☐	hold on to the edge of the cliff		

1 **Match the phrases with the different parts of the stunt. Number the phrases, then say what Kevin has to do.**

First, Kevin has to climb up the building. Then he has to …

2 🎞 ① **Listen and check your answers to Exercise 1.**

3 **Make up your own stunt sequence. Say what Kevin has to do.**

First, he has to climb out of a train, then he has to jump off …

Language focus

Dare devils!

1 **Look at the picture and answer the questions.**

   a Who is David Acton?

   b Who is Anneka?

   c What are they looking at?

2 🔊 ② **Listen to the first part of the programme and check your answers to Exercise 1.**

3 🔊 ③ **Listen to the next part and answer these questions. Write complete sentences.**

   a How many barrels is he going to jump over?

   He's going to jump over …

   b What is he going to do to the barrels first?

   c How fast is he going to ride?

   d How high is he going to jump?

   e How far is he going to jump?

4 🔊 ④ **Listen to the rest of the programme. What happens?**

5 **Work in pairs. Look at the pictures of these other dare devils. What are they going to do?**

FOCUS

going to

- **We can use *going to* to talk about planned actions or intentions in the future.**

  Look at the examples and write two more sentences.

  What's he going to do?

  He's going to jump over the barrels.

- **Anneka gets scared at one point, and says 'He isn't going to jump high enough'.**

  Why does she say that? What can she see? Is she certain?

- **We can also use *going to* when we talk about the future, based on what we see or know in the present.**

6 **In pairs or groups, role-play an interview with Kevin (from Vocabulary) and Anneka. Use your stunt sequence from Exercise 3 of Vocabulary.**

   Anneka What are you going to do first, Kevin?

   Kevin   Well, Anneka, first I'm going to climb out of the train. Then I'm going to jump off …

● Skills focus

Terminal Velocity

Terminal Velocity is an action film starring Charlie Sheen. There are lots of stunts in this film. Here are some pictures of one of them.

This is Ditch, and this is where he is.

This is where he wants to be.

1   **Look at pictures 1 and 2 and read the captions. How is Ditch going to do it? Here are some clues.**

   a   turn the plane over
   b   stand on the wing
   c   sit on the wing
   d   climb on to the wing
   e   hang by the legs

2   **Look at pictures a–e. Match the clues from Exercise 1 with the correct pictures. Be careful – the clues are in the wrong order.**

3   [⌨] ⑤   **Listen to the dialogue. Check your answers to Exercise 2.**

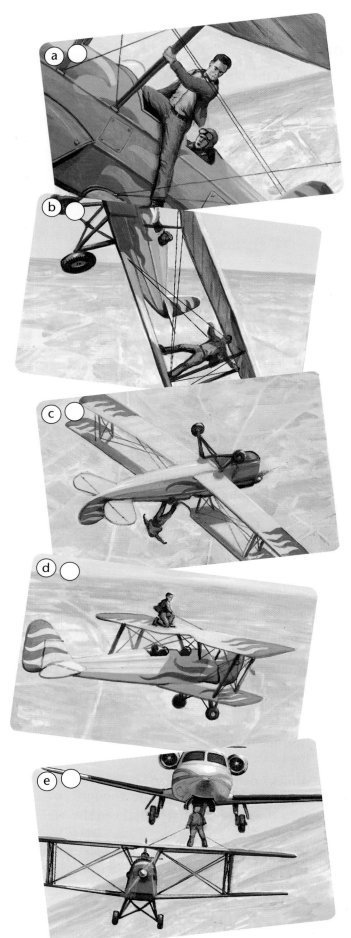

4 Listen again. In your notebook, copy and complete these sentences with Ditch's exact words.

a I'm ..... to ..... out on to the wing.

b I'm ..... to ..... you a signal.

c Then ..... going to turn this plane ..... .

d I'm going to ..... by my legs from the ..... .

e You're ..... turn the ..... back over, right side up.

f Then ..... going to be ..... on the top wing.

g You're ..... next to the other plane.

h I'm ..... climb up the ramp and into the plane.

5 Listen again. Make a note of the pilot's questions.

6 In pairs, act out the dialogue between Ditch and the pilot. Use your answers to Exercises 4 and 5.

Speaking tip 🅡 💬 ◐ 👂

If you think that someone can't hear or understand you when you are talking to them, don't wait for them to tell you. Repeat things or say them in different words. If there's a lot of noise, make sure you say things slowly and clearly, so they can read your lips.

Trapped!

7 Look at the picture. What's happening? Where are the man and the woman?

8 Say what you think they're going to do.

9 Work in pairs. Imagine you are trapped somewhere in the house. Tell your partner where you are, and what you're going to do to get out.

10 Think of another situation and describe it to the class. Your classmates ask you questions to find out how you're going to get out.

Are you going to jump out of the window?
Yes, I am./No, I'm not.

Think about it!

1 This is Daring Delia. She has to do some stunts in a film. What does she have to do?

1  She has to .....
....

2 ....
....

3 ....
....

4 ....
....

2 Write sentences. Use *going to*.

1 Jake / jump / river

....
....

2 Anna and Maria / fall / swimming pool

....
....

3 I / climb / mountain

....
....

4 The girls / get off / bus

....
....

Choose and circle.

😀 Easy   😐 OK   🙁 Difficult

15

SCHOOL LIFE
PEOPLE AND PLACES
FREE TIME
ENTERTAINMENT

Vocabulary

1 Look at the pictures. Complete the labels.

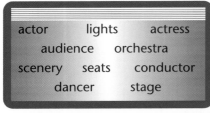

actor   lights   actress
audience   orchestra
scenery   seats   conductor
dancer   stage

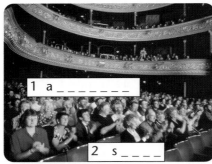

8 l _ _ _ _ _

4 s _ _ _ _ _ _

1 a _ _ _ _ _ _ _

2 s _ _ _ _

10 c _ _ _ _ _ _ _ _

9 d _ _ _ _ _

6 a _ _ _ _ _ _

3 s _ _ _ _

7 a _ _ _ _

5 o _ _ _ _ _ _ _ _

2 🎧 ❶ Listen and check your answers.

3 Now look at the pictures below. Which of these kinds of show do you like?

rock concert   musical   ballet   play

4 Which other kinds of show do you like? Which don't you like? Give reasons.

5 Choose one kind of show from Exercise 3. Talk about what the performers do. Use some of these words and expressions.

shout   wear make-up
sing   look angry/happy
dance   speak their lines
cry   play musical
             instruments

6 Find other phrases with these verbs:

wear   look   play

wear costumes

Language focus

The theatre: past and present

1 **Do you know when and where theatre began? Talk about your ideas.**

2 **Look at the picture and the questions. Then read the text quickly.**

  a Which paragraph tells you about the theatre today?

  b Which paragraph tells you about the theatre in the past?

Nowadays, there are plays and films on television every night, but there are still theatres in most cities where actors perform plays to a live audience. Being part of an audience in a theatre is like being at a football match. Everyone shares the excitement.

Theatre began more than 2,500 years ago in Greece. People sang and danced in the open air to celebrate special days and festivals. At these festivals a chorus of men sang and told stories about gods and heroes. In Greek plays it was easy for the same actors to play many parts because they wore different masks. There were no actresses in those days, and no scenery either.

3 **Read the text again and find out about:**

  a why going to the theatre is like going to see a football match

  b special days and festivals in Greece 2,500 years ago

  c actors nowadays and in the past

  d actresses nowadays and in the past

4 **Look at the questions in Exercise 3. Which are about the present and which are about the past? Which are about the past *and* present? Check that your answers use appropriate tenses.**

5 **Find the past forms of these verbs in the text. Which are irregular?**

  a begin   d tell

  b sing   e wear

  c dance

FOCUS

Contrasting past and present

● **Look at the examples. Complete the sentences about the present.**

Past

Actors wore masks.

There wasn't any scenery.

Women did not act in these plays.

Present

Actors .... masks.

There .... usually scenery.

Women .... in plays today.

Irregular past forms

● **You have to learn irregular past forms. There are no rules, but you can put some of them into groups. For example, these ones all end in –ught:**

Past	Present
brought	bring
bought	buy
caught	catch
taught	teach

6 **Complete the story in your notebook. Use the past tense of the verbs in brackets. Look at the Focus boxes in this unit and in Unit 15 to help you.**

A trip to the theatre

It (be) my birthday last week, and my uncle and aunt (take) me to the theatre. We (see) a play called The Mission. It (be) a really good story, but some of the cast (not speak) their lines very well. In fact, in the first half, an actor (forget) his line and another actor (have to) remind him.

In the second half of the play, part of the scenery (fall down). The audience (begin) to laugh and the actress on stage (look) really angry. Altogether, the actors and actresses (not have) a very good evening. But I really (enjoy) it!

7 🎙️ ❷ **Listen and check your answers.**

8 **Think about the last time you saw a show (in a theatre, on TV, etc.). Describe the show and what happened.**

◉ Skills focus

Theatres around the world

1 **Look at the photo and answer the questions.**

   a Is this a new or an old theatre?

   b Can you name any of the parts you can see?

2 **Read the text and answer the questions.**

   a Who is Britain's most famous playwright?

   b How is the new Globe theatre different from the original one?

Shakespeare and the Globe Theatre

William Shakespeare (1564–1616) is Britain's most famous playwright. In the sixteenth century, people went to see his plays, like *Hamlet* and *Macbeth*, at the Globe Theatre in London. There was no scenery, but he made people believe that the actors were in a forest, on a beach or in a castle, just by the words he used. Women did not act in these plays – teenage boys played female characters like Juliet and Lady Macbeth. Most people stood to watch the play and only the richer people had seats.

The original Globe Theatre burnt down, but today there is a new Globe Theatre in London. It looks exactly like the old one but they can only have plays there in the summer because it is open-air and the weather is too bad in the winter!

3 **Use the text and the photo to write more questions for your partner to answer.**

Was there any scenery?
Where is …?

4 📼 ❸ **You are going to hear Emma's presentation about Eastern Theatre. Listen to the first part.**

   a What are Emma's three questions about?

   b What are the answers to her questions?

5 **Look at the table and the picture. How much information can you fill in just by looking at the picture?**

	Noh theatre
masks	*yes, wooden*
costumes	
wigs	
scenery	
actors	
actresses	
movements	
words	
music	

6 📼 ❹ **Listen and fill in as much of the table as you can. Write short notes like the example.**

7 **Listen again. Can you add any more details?**

8 **Work in pairs. Combine your notes and write a short text about Noh theatre.**

In Noh theatre, the actors wear wooden masks.
They…

9 **Think of a traditional kind of theatre in your country.**

   a Make notes about it.

      ● When did it begin?

      ● Can you still see this kind of theatre?

      ● What is/was it like?

   b Use your notes to give a short presentation to the class.

   c Write a short text based on your presentation.

Dancing in the Street

Calling out, around the world
Are you ready for a brand new beat
Summer's here and the time is right
For dancing in the street
5 Dancing in ......
Down in ......
In ...... City

All we need is music
Sweet music, there'll be music everywhere
10 There'll be swinging, swaying, records playing
Dancing in the street

It doesn't matter what you wear
Just as long as you are there
So, come on, every guy grab a girl
15 Everywhere, around the world

There'll be dancing
Dancing in the street

1 Look at the picture and describe the people.

a Where are they?

b What are they doing?

c How do you think they are feeling?

2   Listen and complete the song. Use these words.

Chicago   New York   New Orleans

3 Think of place names in your own country. Include them in the words of the song and sing your own version.

Think about it!

1 Complete the crossword and find the hidden word.

Across

1 Big painted pictures on stage in a theatre
2 A group of musicians
3 A female actor
4 A type of dance show
5 Without these, you can't see the stage!

The hidden word is: ....

2 Complete the table.

present	past
wear	....
....	caught
buy	....
teach	....

3 What did people do for entertainment before television? Write three things.

They ....
....
....

4 What do you do for entertainment today? Write three things.

I ....
....
....

Choose and circle.

Easy   OK   Difficult

SCHOOL LIFE
PEOPLE AND PLACES
FREE TIME
ENTERTAINMENT

● Vocabulary

> slim   attractive
>
> unfriendly   intelligent   fat
>
> unintelligent   friendly
>
> short   tall   unattractive

1   **Read the adjectives in the box. Which ones can you use to describe:**

   a   appearance?

   b   personality?

2   **Add more adjectives to each group.**

3   **Describe the people in the photographs. Use the following expressions.**

   a   He / She is … [young, tall, attractive, etc.]

   b   He / She has got … [long hair, blue eyes, etc.]

   c   He / She looks … [friendly, intelligent, etc.]

Micky Curtis

Amanda Barrington

4   **Why do we use** *He / She is* **… with some adjectives and** *He / She looks* **… with other adjectives?**

5   **Use the same expressions to describe other story and film characters you know.**

Maxwell   Tara

● Language focus

In Search of the Blue Diamond (part 1)

1 Describe the picture. What is Amanda doing? Where is she?

2 Read the first part of the story and answer the questions.
   a What is Amanda's job?
   b What is her sister's name?
   c Is her sister safe?
   d What does the man on the phone want?

The telephone rang. Amanda stopped typing her novel and picked up the phone nervously.

'Hello?'

'Amanda?'

'Carrie, is that you?' asked Amanda, worriedly.

'Yes, help me! You have to help me …'

'Carrie! Where are you? What's happening?'

There was no answer from her sister. She heard a man's voice.

'Listen very carefully, the man said, calmly. 'We've got your sister. We're going to keep her here until you bring us the Blue Diamond.'

'Blue Diamond? I don't know what you're talking about,' said Amanda.

'We want the Blue Diamond. You've got three days, or you'll never see your sister again!'

3 Find examples of the following forms in the text. Write them in your notebook.
   a past simple – regular verb
   b past simple – irregular verb
   c *will*
   d *going to*
   e present simple
   f present continuous

FOCUS

Telling a story

● When you want to tell a story think about:

   the characters (appearance, personality, how they do things)

   places (where they are, what they're like)

   events and actions (what happened, what people did)

   time (when it happened)

   what people said

● The past simple is one of the forms we can use to talk about events and actions in a story.

   The telephone rang. Amanda stopped typing …

Adverbs

● Adverbs often tell us how the characters did things, or how they felt when they did them.

● As you read the story in this unit, find more examples of adverbs. Which two letters do a lot of adverbs end in?

4 Look at these pictures. What do you think is going to happen in the story? Make a note of your ideas.

Amanda is going to travel by plane.

She's going to …

● Skills focus

In Search of the Blue Diamond (part 2)

1   Amanda put the phone down and looked at the map on her desk. She only had half of the map. It showed the first part of the route to Devil's Island, in the middle of the
5   Borinoco River. She knew the diamond was in a cave on the island, but she didn't know how to get there.

Ten hours later she arrived in Moronia. She knew she had to get to Cartawaya, but how?
10   She saw a woman outside the airport. The woman looked friendly, so Amanda asked her politely about transport. The woman pointed to a yellow taxi. Amanda got in the taxi and gave the name of the first town on
15   the map. The driver looked surprised because it was a long way away. Amanda repeated the name clearly, and showed him some money. 'OK,' he said, and started the car.
20   They got to the only hotel in Cartawaya late in the evening. Amanda checked in and went to her room. She was too tired to eat. She went to sleep immediately.

Next morning, the weather was brilliant. She
25   decided to have breakfast on the terrace. There were only two other people there, a fat

man in a suit and a beautiful woman. Amanda recognized the woman from the airport. She drank her coffee and took the
30   map out of her bag. When she looked up again, the man wasn't there. Suddenly she felt cold metal against her neck and heard a man's voice. 'Leave the map on the table and move slowly.' Amanda stood up. She
35   was really scared. And then it was over. The fat man fell back against the wall. She turned around and saw a different man – a young man – holding the gun.

'Get your map and run!' he shouted. 'I've
40   got the other half!'

* * * *

It was early afternoon. The sun was high in the sky, and the air was hot. Amanda took out the map. She looked around carefully. There were mountains to the left, and a
45   swamp to the right. She saw a large, heart-shaped rock in front of her. She checked her map excitedly. There it was! The heart-shaped rock! Now she had to decide which road to take. She turned to her new friend.
50   'Are you coming with me, or not?'

1   Read the story quickly and find the answers to these questions.

a   Which country does Amanda fly to?

b   Which places does she visit and when?

2   Read the story again more slowly. Work out the answers to these questions and give reasons.

a   What was the cold metal against her neck?

b   Why did the fat man fall back against the wall? What happened?

3   Find the simple past of these irregular verbs in the story. Write the line numbers.

drink	☐	go	☐	put	☐1
feel	☐	have to	☐	see	☐
get	☐	hear	☐	stand	☐
give	☐	know	☐	take	☐

4   Put these events into the correct order.

a   Amanda has a cup of coffee.

b   Amanda finds the heart-shaped rock.

c   Amanda takes a taxi to a hotel.

d   Amanda gets a phone call.

e   Amanda leaves the hotel with a young man.

f   Amanda travels to Moronia.

5   Write a paragraph to summarize the story so far. Use your answers to Exercises 1–4. Begin like this.

First, Amanda gets a phone call. Then she …

> **Look!**
>
> We normally use the past simple for the events in a story when we are writing it.
>
> *but*
>
> We can use the present simple when we are talking about the story.

6 What do you think is going to happen next? Discuss it in your groups. Use the following expressions to make suggestions and to agree or disagree.

I think they're going to …

So do I!

Neither do I.

I think so, too.

Really? I don't agree.

7 Listen to the end of the story. Compare it with your group's ideas.

Reading tip

If you're reading for pleasure, don't stop to look up every new word in a dictionary. If you can follow the story, keep reading. (If you can do Exercise 4, that means you can follow this story.)

Think about it!

1 Complete the words.

1 She looks
i _ _ _ _ _ _ _ _ _ _ .

2 He is t _ _ _ and
s _ _ _ _ .

3 It looks
u n _ _ _ _ _ _ _ _ _ .

4 She thinks she's very
a t _ _ _ _ _ _ _ _ _ .

2 Complete the text. Write the verbs in the past simple.

Mick ¹............. (walk) into the hotel. He ²............. (have) no luggage. He ³............. (check) in to the hotel and ⁴............. (go) to his room. When he ⁵............. (get) there, he ⁶............. (hear) a noise. He ⁷............. (turn) round quickly and ⁸............. (see) a man with a gun. 'Help,' Mick ⁹............. (shout). The man ¹⁰............. (point) the gun at him and ¹¹............. (say), 'Remember me?'

3 What do you think happened next? Write your ideas in your notebook.

Choose and circle.

Easy   OK   Difficult

Revision

Units 1–5

Stop and think!

- Do the exercises on pages 24–27. Start with section A, 'Question words'.
- Look at the HELP screens if you need more practice.

A	Question words	OK	HELP
B	Food	OK	HELP
C	*going to*	OK	HELP
D	Adverbs	OK	HELP
E	Irregular verbs	OK	HELP

- Colour each letter when you can do the section.

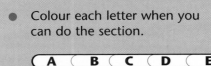

Well done!

A
- Look at the Focus box on page 5.
- Read item 3 of the Grammar Summary in *Brainwaves 2*.
- Practise asking and answering with a partner.

B
- Look at the pictures on page 8.
- Read item 4 of the Grammar Summary in *Brainwaves 2*.
- Do Workbook Unit 2 Exercise 1.

C
- Look at the Focus box on page 13.
- Read item 12 of the Grammar Summary in *Brainwaves 2*.
- Do Workbook Unit 3 Exercises 4–5.

D
- Look at the Focus box on page 21.
- Read item 3 of the Grammar Summary.
- Read the story again on page 22.

E
- Look at the Focus box on page 17.
- Read item 1 of the Grammar Summary.
- Do Workbook Unit 4 Buzz words.

Question words

1 Complete the questions Tom's friend asks him about his weekend by adding the correct question word(s).

Friend	.... did you go on Saturday?
Tom	I went to Manchester to watch a football match.
Friend	.... did you go with?
Tom	I went with my brother and his friend, Mick.
Friend	.... is it from here to Manchester?
Tom	It's about 120 kilometres.
Friend	.... did you get there?
Tom	We went in my brother's car.
Friend	.... did it take?
Tom	About two hours.

Friend	.... you enjoy the game?
Tom	Yes, it was very exciting.
Friend	.... was the score?
Tom	3–0 to Manchester United.
Friend	.... they your favourite team?
Tom	Yes, they are.
Friend	.... you go and see them again?
Tom	Yes, I'm sure we will.
Friend	.... your brother got room for one more person in his car?
Tom	Yes, I think so.
Friend	.... I come with you next time?
Tom	Of course, Tom – if you support Manchester United!

2 Ask your friend about what he or she did last weekend. Make notes and report back to the class.

● B Food

1 Look at the picture. Complete and answer the questions.

1 <u>How much</u>............ does a kilo of potatoes cost?
....

2 .... eggs can you buy with £2.40?
....

3 .... does a chicken cost?
....

4 .... do three kilos of onions cost?
....

5 .... bottles of oil can you get for £2.70? ....

6 .... cheese can you get for £2.50?
....

2 Look at the dishes below. What are they made with? Complete the diagram and draw some more in your notebook for the other dishes.

curry   cake   omelette   pizza

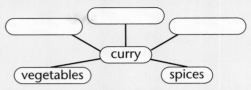

3 Choose a dish. Write sentences in your notebook about what it is made with, filled with and served with. Show them to your partner. Can he or she tell what the dish is?

● C going to

1 Make sentences using *going to* and match them with the pictures.

1 He / set fire to the house.   *d*
   <u>He's going to set fire to the house.</u>

2 The dogs / attack him.   .....
   ....

3 She / not / dive into the pool.   .....
   ....

4 They / not / sunbathe today.   .....
   ....

5 He / break the glass.   .....
   ....

2 Sara is going to spend a week in California. Write the questions her friend asks her.

you/stay/big hotel?

Are you going to stay in a big hotel?

1 you/visit/Hollywood?

.... ?

2 your sister/travel with you?

.... ?

3 you/swim/in the sea?

.... ?

4 you/look for/film stars?

....?

5 you/go/surfing?

.... ?

D Adverbs

1 Complete the table.

adjective	adverb
slow	
worried	
calm	
	carefully
polite	
	nervously
immediate	

2 Complete the sentences with an adverb from the table in Exercise 1.

1 'Oh dear, I hope everything is going to be all right,' she said, ...

2 'Don't worry,' he said, ... 'Everything is under control.'

3 A strange noise came from the dark, empty room. She opened the door ....

4 'Excuse me. Could you please move to your left a little?' she asked, ...

5 I was so tired that I went to sleep ....

6 Think .... before you make any important decisions.

E Irregular verbs

1 Put the verbs in brackets into the past simple.

The last time we [1]............... (go) for a picnic it was a disaster. First of all, Dad [2]............... (forget) to put petrol in the car and we [3]............... (have to) walk for miles to find a garage. Then it [4]............... (take) hours to find the picnic spot. We finally [5]............... (stop) under a tree next to a river and [6]............... (begin) to get the food out of the car. We all [7]............... (sit) under the tree and [8]............ (drink) tea while Dad [9]............... (make) a fire to heat the food on. Unfortunately, Dad [10]............... (burn) himself with the matches. My sister and I decided to go for a walk in the fields, but she [11]............... (stand) on a snake and we both [12]............... (run) back, very scared. We [13]............. (tell) Mum and Dad, and they both [14]............... (get) very upset.

We decided it [15]............... (be) too dangerous to stay in that place, and [16]............... (put) all our things back in the car. 'Wait a minute,' [17]............. (say) Mum, 'I want to wash my hands in the river.' We all [18]............... (hear) a big splash, and [19]............... (see) Mum climb out of the river, soaking wet. 'I [20]............... (know) that would happen!', said Dad, and [21]............... (give) her a towel. 'I hope you [22]............... (bring) a change of clothes!'

● Reading and writing

1 Ralph is on holiday in Australia. Read the letter
he wrote to his friend. Then look at the
sentences below and put the correct sentence –
A, B, C, D or E – in the gaps in the letter.

Dear Bill

*1 ..... The flight wasn't late, but 36 hours on a plane is a
long time! I'm writing this letter from my hotel room, which
is very nice.*

*2 ...... Every room has a TV, and its own bathroom — and
the beds are very comfortable. Everyone that works here is
very polite and helpful, and the restaurant serves great
food. If we ever come to Australia again, we will definitely
come back to this place.*

*3 ...... First, we went to the famous Sydney Opera House.
Then we had lunch in a lovely little bar in the city. In the
afternoon we took a ferry to Bondi Beach and sunbathed
until six o'clock. When we finally got back, we were so tired
we went straight to bed.*

*4 ...... We want to travel all along the south coast by train.
We have only got three weeks to do this, so we are going to
have to hurry! Our train leaves at 8.30 tomorrow morning.*

*5 ...... I'm going to bed because I'm exhausted — having fun is
such hard work! I'll write to you when we get to Adelaide.*

Best wishes

Ralph

A Tomorrow, we are going to leave Sydney.
B We arrived in Sydney two nights ago and I'm
   still very tired.
C Well, that's all for now.
D We had quite an exciting day yesterday.
E We were quite surprised at how nice the hotel is.

2 **Imagine you are having the holiday of your
dreams. Make notes about:**
   ● your arrival
   ● the hotel
   ● what you did yesterday
   ● what you are going to do

3 **Use your notes from Exercise 2 to write a letter
to a friend, telling him or her about your
holiday.**

● Project idea

● Make your own 'skyscraper sandwich', using
pictures from magazines or your own
drawings.
● Display your sandwich and describe it to the
class.
● As a class, have a competition to decide which
one is:
   ● the most delicious
   ● the biggest
   ● the most colourful
   ● the most original
   ● the most disgusting

Vocabulary

SCHOOL LIFE
PEOPLE AND PLACES
FREE TIME
ENTERTAINMENT

COME TO THE CLUBS AND SOCIETIES FAIR!

Next Tuesday at 4 o'clock in the school hall.

Find out about all the different clubs and societies at the school.

Talk to other students about how to join.

Here are some of the clubs and societies which will be at the fair.

The penfriends club

The drama society

The music society

jewellery

chess

The sports and games club

The arts and crafts club

coins

stamps

dolls

The collectors' club

badges

1 Look at the poster.

   a What event is it advertising?

   b When and where is the event taking place?

2 What can people do at these clubs and societies? Use the words below, then add ideas of your own.

collect do go make play practise	aerobics an instrument badges chess coins football horse-riding jewellery models stamps

3 Which of the clubs and societies would you like to join? Why?

I'd like to join the collectors' club because I'm interested in collecting coins.

I wouldn't like to join the sports and games club because I don't like sport.

4 What other things are you interested in? Find out if anyone else in the class has the same hobby.

ice-skating   folk dancing   gymnastics

● Language focus

Joining the music society

1 Look at the photo and answer the questions.

a What kind of society do you think this is?

b What activities do you think take place at the society?

c What do you think the boy and girl are talking about?

2 🎹❶ **Listen and check your ideas.**

3 Listen again. Tick (✓) the correct column.

	have to/ need to	don't have to
be able to play an instrument	☐	☐
pay a fee	☐	☐
fill in a form	☐	☐
bring CDs or cassettes	☐	☐
sing a song	☐	☐

4 Work in pairs or groups. Choose a hobby.

a Make a chart like this.

	have to/ need to	don't have to
have a bike	✔	
wear special clothes		✔
be very fit		✔
enjoy exercise	✔	

b Tell the class what is or isn't necessary for your hobby. Your classmates guess what your hobby is.

FOCUS

need to/have to/ don't have to

● **Look at the examples and answer the questions.**

You need to fill in this form.
You have to sing a song.
You don't have to pay a fee.

a Is it necessary to fill in a form?

b Is it necessary to sing a song?

c Is it necessary to pay a fee?

● **Now complete these sentences with *have to*, *don't have to*, and *need to*.**

We can use .... or ....
for things which are necessary. We can use
.... for things which aren't necessary.

● **Use your answers to Exercise 3 to talk about what is or isn't necessary for joining the music society.**

You need to/have to …
You don't have to …

● Skills focus

What's your hobby?

1 Read the text below and look at the photos. What are the letters going to be about?

Some members of the Penfriends Club write about their hobbies in their letters, and send photos to their penfriends. Here are extracts from two letters.

2 Work in pairs or groups A and B. Copy the table into your notebook, then follow steps a–d.

a **Group A:** Cover letter B. Read the first sentence of letter A and choose the right photo.
Now read the whole letter and make notes in the table.

Group B: Cover letter A. Read the first sentence of letter B and choose the right photo.
Now read the whole letter and make notes in the table.

b **Group A:** Use your notes to tell B about your letter.

His hobby is collecting … For this hobby, you need to/have to … but you needn't/don't have to …

Group B: Listen and make notes in the table.

c **Group B:** Use your notes to tell A about your letter.

Her hobby is painting … For this hobby, you need to/have to … but you needn't/don't have to …

Group A: Listen and make notes in the table.

d Now read the other letter. Complete your notes if necessary.

	letter A	letter B
hobby		
when started		
how/why started		
you need to/have to		
you needn't/don't have to		
cheap/expensive		

A

My hobby is collecting stones. I started collecting them when I was eight. We lived in a town by the sea, and I found lots of different stones on the beach.

I clean and polish them, and then I find out what kind of stones they are. I've got lots of books about geology. I display the stones on shelves, each with a label saying what kind of stone it is, and when and where I found it. Altogether, I've got 250 stones in my collection.

It's a good hobby because you don't have to spend money. You only need to buy the books and ask someone to build some shelves!

3 Write a letter about a hobby of your own.

a Use the headings from the table in Exercise 2 to make notes about your hobby.

b Use your notes to write 3 paragraphs.

Paragraph 1
  Introduce your hobby.

Paragraph 2
  Say what is or isn't necessary for the hobby.

Paragraph 3
  Say why you think it's a good hobby.

c Read each other's letters. Which do you find most interesting?

Look!

You don't have to spend a lot of money.
=
You needn't spend a lot of money.

B

In my spare time, I paint designs on T-shirts. I got the idea two years ago for my brother's birthday present. The shop wanted £20 for a special design on a T-shirt, so I decided to do it myself. I bought a white cotton T-shirt for £6 and some paints, and I painted a lion on the front. My brother loved it!

Painting T-shirts is great fun. You needn't be a great artist, you can just paint shapes and lines. The T-shirts are the most expensive part of my hobby. You have to use special fabric paints – but they last a long time, so they're not really expensive – and you need to buy good quality brushes.

I love my hobby because you can make T-shirts that no-one else has got. I give a lot of them away as presents to my family and friends. Sometimes, I sell them. Since I started, I've made about 60 T-shirts and each one is different.

Think about it!

1 Match the pictures with the hobbies and interests below.

a make jewellery ..3..   d collect stamps ......

b play chess ......   e do aerobics ......

c go horse-riding ......

2 Name more hobbies and interests. Use the verbs from Exercise 1.

a make   models, badges.

b play   ....

c go   ....

d collect ....

e do   ....

3 Complete these sentences about being a good student. Use *need to* or *needn't*.

a You ...need to... work hard.

b You .... listen to your teachers.

c You .... be rich.

d You .... do your homework.

e You .... have a lot of money.

4 Write more sentences about being a good student. Use *have to* or *don't have to*.

You don't have to live in a big city.

....

....

....

....

Choose and circle.

Easy   OK   Difficult

● Vocabulary

1

2

3

4

5

6

7

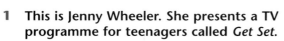

8

9

1 **This is Jenny Wheeler. She presents a TV programme for teenagers called *Get Set*.**

a Where is Jenny in each photo? Use these words:

studio   restaurant   wardrobe department
office   kitchen   entrance   bathroom
on the set   dressing room

b How did you work out the meaning of each word? Read and tick the techniques you used, then add any ideas of your own.

I knew the word already. ☐

The word is the same or similar in my own language. ☐

I knew part of the word. ☐

It was the only word left. ☐

2 **Describe the photos.**

It's early in the morning. She's eating breakfast.

3 **Look at these phrases. *Have* can mean different things.**

a Think of an equivalent for each phrase.

have breakfast = eat breakfast
have a discussion = talk about (or discuss) something

have ➤	breakfast
	lunch
	a meal

| have ➤ | a meeting |
| | a discussion |

have ➤	a cup of coffee
	a cup of tea
	a drink

| have ➤ | a rest |
| | a shower |

b Describe the pictures again. Use phrases with *have* where you can.

4 **Think about your own daily routine.**

a In your notebook, copy and make notes in the table.

Time	Place	Activity
in the morning	at home	brush my teeth, have a shower …
	at school	
in the afternoon		
in the evening		

b Use your notes to talk about your daily routine.

In the morning, I brush my teeth, I have a shower and … . Then, I …

● Language focus

Comic Relief's Red Nose Day

1 Look at the photos. Is this a normal day for Jenny? What's different?

2 Read the captions (1–5) and match them with the photos. Say what helped you to match them.

a 2

b ☐

c ☐

d ☐

e ☐

Once every two years in Britain, the charity Comic Relief holds Red Nose Day. People wear red noses and do silly things to collect money. The charity uses the money to fight poverty in the UK and Africa. Jenny wrote a photo article about Red Nose Day for a magazine.

1 Last Thursday was Red Nose Day. I didn't have a very good start – I was really late for work. I missed my bus, and arrived at the TV centre at 9.30. It's not like me – I usually arrive before 9 o'clock. I didn't even have time to talk to Eddie, the security guard.

2 I ran straight to the dressing room, and put on my clown outfit. Thank goodness I didn't have to iron it first! Normally, I wear my own clothes, and I always have to iron them. But this was a special day. I must admit I felt a bit silly with a red nose, but everyone else had one too!

3 I just had enough time to have a light lunch. I decided to have a salad, because it's quick. Usually I have a cooked meal. But what a surprise when I got there! Everything was red! It was horrible to look at, but it still tasted good.

4 After our usual rehearsal, I went on to the set and started the programme, and began an interview with actor Chet Walker, my guest for the day. I normally sit in a comfortable armchair, but today the director wanted me to sit on a plastic chair. I soon found out why. Suddenly, at the end of the interview the director came in and covered me in gunge! Yuk! What a mess! But I collected a LOT of money for charity from the people in the studio for that!

5 At the end of the programme, I needed a shower! I normally have a cup of tea and then go home, but this was Red Nose Day, so we had a special office party. We all wore our red noses, of course. I think our producer looks better with a red nose – what do you think?

3 Read the captions again, and make notes about Jenny's normal day and her unusual day. Make a table like this in your notebook.

normal day	unusual day
arrives at work before 9.00	*arrived late*

Present simple and past simple

● Look at your table from Exercise 3.

  a Which verb form did you use for her normal day? Write an example.

  b Which verb form did you use for her unusual day last week? Write an example.

● Look at the example below. How do we form the past simple of regular verbs?

  I missed my bus.

  Base form + ...

● What about irregular verbs?

  a Match these verbs and past forms.

run	was
be	got
feel	ran
have	put
put	felt
get	had

  b Find more irregular verbs in the text in Exercise 2 and add them to the list.

4 Use your notes from Exercise 3 to talk about Jenny's normal day and her unusual day.

She usually arrives before 9.00, but on Red Nose Day she arrived late.

5 Think about a special or unusual day at your school, for example, a sports day.

  a Make notes about this unusual day and your normal day.

  b Use you notes to tell your partner about your unusual day, comparing it with your normal day.

  c Write a short article about it. Use Jenny's article to help you. Add pictures or drawings if you like.

Skills focus

An interview with Chet Walker

1 Look at the photo. Where is Jenny? What is she doing?

2 📻 **①** Read questions a–c. Then listen to the first part of the interview and answer the questions.

  a Where does Chet Walker live?

  b What did he do last month?

  c What is the rest of the interview going to be about?

> **Look!**
>
> 🇺🇸 movie = 🇬🇧 film

3 Listen again.

  a In your notebooks make notes about Chet's normal life, and what he did last month.

normally	last month
goes to school	*made a movie*

  b Use your notes to compare Chet's normal life with what he did last month.

  He normally goes to school every day, but last month was different. He spent every day in the studio …

4 You're going to listen to the rest of the interview. What do you think Jenny is going to ask Chet about? Complete these questions.

  a ..... spend much time with your friends?

  b ..... work in the evenings?

  c ..... make any new friends when you're filming?

  d ..... a lot of money?

  e ..... travel a lot?

5 📻 **②** Listen to the rest of the interview.

  a Check your ideas for Exercise 4.

  b Listen again. Make a note of Chet's answers.

  c Make notes about the advantages and disadvantages of Chet's life as a film star.

advantages	disadvantages

6 Role-play an interview. Student A is the film star, Student B is the interviewer.

Student A

Complete a fact file about yourself. Make up the information or choose a film star you know about. Use the information to give your answers.

> Name:
> Age:
> Home:
> First film:
> Most recent film:
> Advantages of being a film star:
>
> Disadvantages of being a film star:

Student B

Use the questions from Exercise 4 and add your own ideas. You can ask about:

home   friends   money   travel   work

Introduce your guest, then start the interview!

7 Work in groups.

a Think about the advantages and disadvantages of being famous. Use your notes from Exercise 5c and add your own ideas.

b Read the following expressions, and add any more expressions you know.

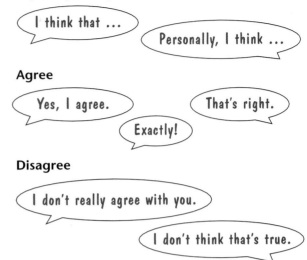

Express your opinions

I think that ...

Personally, I think ...

Agree

Yes, I agree.

That's right.

Exactly!

Disagree

I don't really agree with you.

I don't think that's true.

c Discuss your ideas. What is your conclusion? Is being famous a good thing or a bad thing?

Think about it!

1 Complete the sentences with these words.

drink   ~~breakfast~~   lunch   rest   discussion

a I usually have ..breakfast.. at 7.30.

b My teachers had a .... about my work.

c We always have .... in the school canteen.

d I normally have a .... with my food.

e Sometimes, I need to have a .... when I get home.

2 Write the past simple of these verbs.

Present	Past
arrive	arrived
go	went
run	....
decide	....
feel	....
collect	....

3 Look at the verbs in Exercise 2. Which ones are irregular?

....

4 Write two sentences about what you do every day.

I always have breakfast. ....

....

....

5 Now write two sentences about what you did yesterday.

Yesterday, I phoned my friend. ....

....

....

6 Look at the verbs in your answers to Exercises 4 and 5. Which tense did you use for:

a something you always, or usually, do?

....

b something different from your normal routine? ....

Choose and circle.

Easy   OK   Difficult

SCHOOL LIFE
PEOPLE AND PLACES
FREE TIME
ENTERTAINMENT

Vocabulary

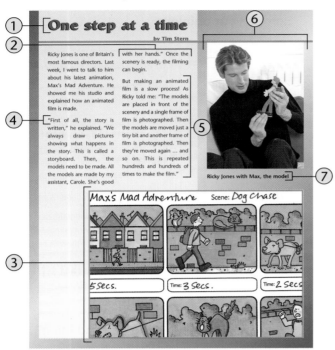

① **One step at a time**

② by Tim Stern

④ Ricky Jones is one of Britain's most famous directors. Last week, I went to talk to him about his latest animation, Max's Mad Adventure. He showed me his studio and explained how an animated film is made.

"First of all, the story is written," he explained. "We always draw pictures showing what happens in the story. This is called a storyboard. Then, the models need to be made. All the models are made by my assistant, Carole. She's good with her hands." Once the scenery is ready, the filming can begin.

But making an animated film is a slow process! As Ricky told me: "The models are placed in front of the scenery and a single frame of film is photographed. Then the models are moved just a tiny bit and another frame of film is photographed. Then they're moved again ... and so on. This is repeated hundreds and hundreds of times to make the film."

⑥ ⑤
Ricky Jones with Max, the model ⑦

Max's Mad Adventure   Scene: Dog Chase
5 secs.   Time: 3 secs.   Time: 2 secs ③

1 Look at the picture of a magazine page.
   a Who do you think reads this kind of magazine?
   b What kinds of magazine do you like? Why?

2 Find these features on the magazine page. Write the correct number next to each word.

caption ☑7 column ☐ heading ☐
illustration ☐ paragraph ☐ photo ☐
line ☐

3 Look at the photos of the people who work on this magazine. Say what you think they are doing.

1 Lisa Ryan, editor

2 Amanda Cooke, designer

3 Tim Stern, reporter

4 Rebecca Farrell, picture researcher

4 Read these job descriptions, and match them to the people. Say what helped you to match them.

a I spend a lot of time out of the office, interviewing people. When I get back to the office with my notes, I **key** (type) my story into the computer. Then I give the **copy**, or text, to the editor for checking.

....

b When the reporters bring their stories, I read them and choose which ones to use in the magazine. Then I **edit** the texts – this means that I check them for mistakes and make any necessary changes. Finally, I pass the copy and the photos to the designer in the art department.

....

c I work in the art department, and my job is to choose photos to use with the stories. Usually, a photographer brings in several photos, but sometimes I have to contact a **picture library**. This is a special kind of library where they keep thousands of photos of different people, places, and things.

....

d I work on a computer most of the time. I design the **layout** of the pages, that is, what they will look like. I arrange the text, photos, and headings. When it's all done, I print the pages out from the computer. These print-outs are called **proofs**. I send them to the printers, and then I start thinking about the next issue of the magazine!

....

5 Read the descriptions again and work out the meaning of the words in bold. Then say which technique (a–d) you used for each word.
   a There is a synonym, in brackets or commas, after the word.
   b The next few words explain the meaning.
   c The next sentence explains the meaning.
   d The previous part of the sentence explains the meaning.

   'Key' means 'type'. There's a synonym in brackets after the word - technique 'a'.

6 Which person's job do you think is the most interesting? The most creative? The least interesting? Explain your answers.

Language focus

How a magazine is produced

1 **Look at the chart above. What does it show?**

2 **Read the captions below and put them into the correct order.**

a Photographs are chosen and the layout is designed on the computer. ☐

b The stories are edited and passed on to the art department. ☐

c The film is sent to the printers. ☐

d The magazine is printed, packed, and distributed to shops. ☐

e The stories are keyed into the computer, and then passed on to the editor. ☐

f The pages are printed out on to a special film. ☐

3 **This chart shows some of the stages of book production. Use the pictures and the words to describe the process.**

pages/print *The pages are printed.*

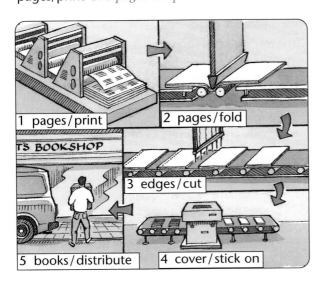

1 pages/print

2 pages/fold

3 edges/cut

4 cover/stick on

5 books/distribute

FOCUS

Present passive

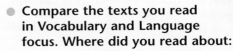

● **Compare the texts you read in Vocabulary and Language focus. Where did you read about:**

a the people who produce the magazine?

....

b the process/stages of producing the magazine?

....

● **Look at the verb forms in the following sentence. We can choose this form to talk about what and how something is done. Here, we are describing the stages of a process.**

Photographs <u>are chosen</u> and the layout <u>is designed</u> on the computer.

● **Find more examples of this form (*be* + past participle) in the captions in Exercise 2.**

● **Verbs have got three parts. Look at the examples:**

	Base form	Past simple	Past participle
Regular verbs	design	designed	designed
Irregular verbs	choose	chose	chosen

● **Find more past participles in the captions and add them to a chart in your notebooks. Complete the base forms and the past forms.**

4 **Use what you have learned in this unit to talk about what happens with the illustrations and text *before* the pages of a book are printed.**

Skills focus

How an animated film is made

1   Tim Stern is interviewing Ricky Jones, a film director. Look at the photo and try to answer the questions.

a   What kind of film does Ricky Jones direct?

b   Who is Max?

2    ① Look at the chart below. Who does each thing, Ricky or somebody else? Listen to the interview and tick (✓) the correct column.

	Ricky	somebody else
write the story		
make the models		
paint the scenery		
operate the camera		
move the models		
record the voices		
add the sound effects		

3   Try to complete Tim's notes. Then listen to the interview again and check your answers.

The story is written .... by a team of writers.

.... by Carole, Ricky's assistant.

.... by Nigel, the sound effects man.

.... by actors.

.... by the cameraman.

.... by artists.

.... by Carole, Ricky's assistant.

4   Write Tim Stern's report for the magazine. Use your answers to Exercise 3 to help you. Start like this:

I went to visit Ricky Jones, the film director, to find out how an animated film is made. First, the story is written. Next, …

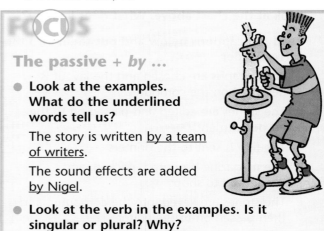

FOCUS

The passive + *by* …

● **Look at the examples. What do the underlined words tell us?**

The story is written <u>by a team of writers</u>.

The sound effects are added <u>by Nigel</u>.

● **Look at the verb in the examples. Is it singular or plural? Why?**

Game

1   **Work in pairs or groups. You are going to play a game called *Max's Mad Adventure*.**

a   You will need a dice or spinner, at least ten pieces of paper, and one counter per player.

b   Write each of the ten prompts below on a separate piece of paper.

chase/dog	win/car
trap/indoors/storm	buy/bicycle
bite/mosquito	find/horse
frighten/tiger	meet/friend
send/to bed/doctor	have/meal

The first five prompts are bad things which happen to you in the game. If they happen, you miss your next go.

chase/dog = *You are chased by a dog. Miss a go!*

The other five prompts are good things. If they happen, you have an extra go.

win/car = *You win a car. Throw again!*

Think of more prompts for good and bad things, and write them on pieces of paper.

2   **Play the game.**

a   Take it in turns to throw the dice. If you land on a square with a question mark (?), another player picks up a piece of paper and makes a sentence.

b   The winner is the first player to reach the finish.

Think about it!

1 Look back through this unit. Find at least one example of these things. Write the page number.

a a photo ....

b an illustration ....

c a heading.........................

d a caption..........................

2 Write sentences in the passive about producing a magazine.

a stories/write

   The stories are written.

b text/check

   ....

c pictures/choose

   ....

d pages/design

   ....

3 Who does each of the stages (a–d) in Exercise 2?

   editor .... designer .... reporter ....
   picture researcher ....

4 Write the past participles of these verbs.

   write   *written*   choose ....

   make   ....   send   ....

   move   ....

5 Look back through the unit. Find three more verbs and their past participles.

   ....

   ....

Choose and circle.

Easy   OK   Difficult

SCHOOL LIFE
PEOPLE AND PLACES
FREE TIME
ENTERTAINMENT

🌀 Vocabulary

1   Look at the picture and read the text.

a   What is the difference between an active and an inactive volcano?

b   Look at the gaps in the text. What kind of words are missing: nouns, verbs, or adjectives?

c   Think of a word which can fill each gap. In each case, try to find a word which makes sense when you read the whole sentence.

2   🎧 ❶ Listen and fill in the gaps with the words you hear, then check with your teacher. Compare the words on tape with your own ideas from Exercise 1c.

a   Which words are the same?

b   Which words have a similar meaning, but are not the same?

c   Which words are completely different? Do you still think your word makes sense?

Volcanoes are named after Vulcan, the Roman god of fire. Most volcanoes are inactive, but an active volcano can suddenly become a mountain of fire. When a volcano erupts, the lava and ash can ¹..... towns and villages, and ²..... the people who live there.

The first well-recorded eruption was that of Vesuvius in AD 79. It ³..... the Roman towns of Pompeii and Herculaneum, and ⁴..... 16,000 people. A Roman writer, Pliny the Younger, ⁵..... the eruption. He ⁶.... about the 'horrible black cloud' and 'sudden flashes, larger than lightning'.

3   Look at the picture of Herculaneum. Is it a modern town or a town in the past? How do you know?

4   What are the people in the picture doing?

a   Match these words to the people numbered 1–6 in the picture. Write sentences in your notebook.

a   woman / feed / chickens
b   girl / pick / grapes
c   fisherman / mend / nets
d   women / carry / jugs of water
e   potter / make / bowl
f   man / mend / wheel

1   A fisherman is mending his nets.

b   Now talk about the other people and the animals in the picture.

A cat is sleeping.

Pronunciation

5   🎧 ❷ Listen to the sentences from Exercise 4a.

a   Check the answers in your notebook. Correct them if necessary.

b   Listen again and mark the stresses in each sentence.

A fisherman is mending his nets.

c   Look at your answers. Why are these words stressed? Repeat the sentences.

● Language focus

A tour of Herculaneum

1   ❸   **Listen to the first part of the tape. What is Juliet's job?**

2   **Look at part of a plan of Herculaneum.**

   a What can you see in each room?

   b Where can you normally find these things?

     You find toys in a bedroom.

     You find pots and pans…

   c What are these things used for?

     Pots and pans are used for cooking.

3   ❹   **Listen to the rest of the tour. In which order do they visit the rooms? Number them 1–3 on the plan.**

4   **Look at the first room they visit on the plan.**

   a Fill in the gaps in the text.

   b Listen to Juliet again and check your answers.

   Here we are in the first room. As you can see, this was probably the home of a young man and his wife. If we look at their bodies, and the other objects in the room, we can work out what they were ¹…… when Vesuvius erupted. We found a ²…… next to the man, and some ³…… and ⁴…… near the woman. At the time of the eruption, the man was ⁵…… a wheel and his wife was ⁶…… dinner.

5   **You are going to continue the tour of Herculaneum.**

   a Look at the second and third rooms on the plan and make notes.

   b Listen to Juliet and add to your notes if necessary.

   c Continue the tour. Describe the two rooms and say what the people were doing. Add any other ideas of your own.

6   **Look at the picture of Herculaneum on the Vocabulary page. Say what other people were doing at the time of the eruption.**

   When Vesuvius erupted, the girl was picking grapes.

FOCUS

Past continuous – interrupted past

● **Look at the diagram. Which sentence is in the past simple?**

Vesuvius erupted.

The man was mending a wheel.

● **The other sentence is in the past continuous. How do we form this tense? Complete:**

past continuous = the past of ……………… + the –*ing* form of the verb

● **Complete this sentence about the use of the past simple and past continuous.**

We can use the past ……………… to describe a continuous action in the past. We use the past ……………… for an event which interrupts that continuous action.

Skills focus

Earthquake!

1 Look at the picture of Sarah Cox and try to answer the questions.

a What is her job?

b Why is she in Northridge, California?

2 🔲 **5** Listen and check your ideas.

3 🔲 **6** Which three people did Sarah Cox interview? Listen and tick (✓) the correct names.

Rob King	✓	Malcolm Jones	☐
Hannah Green	☐	Helen Smith	☐
Marc Peel	☐	Antonio Gonzales	☐
Simon Moore	☐	Ted Willis	☐

4 What were they doing when the earthquake started? Listen again and make notes in the table.

	who?	at time of earthquake ...
a	Rob King	mending bike
b	his brother	
c	....	
d	her husband	
e	....	
f	his children	

5 Use your notes from Exercise 4. Make complete sentences about what they were doing at the time of the earthquake.

Rob King was mending his bike.

His brother ...

6 Imagine you were in Northridge at the time of the earthquake. What were you doing? What were other people in your family doing? Make a list.

7 In pairs, role-play an interview with a news reporter and an inhabitant of Northridge. Use these expressions to help you.

What were you doing when ... ?

When the earthquake started, I was ...

What was your ... doing?

He / She was ...

What were your ... doing?

They were ...

What happened then?

I ...

8 Help Sarah Cox complete her article.

a Read the first paragraph of the article and look at your notes from Exercise 4. Is the information the same?

b Read the second paragraph. Use your notes from Exercise 4 to complete the missing information.

c Continue the third paragraph. Write about the characters you invented for the role-play in Exercises 6 and 7.

Quake shakes the valley

This morning, San Fernando valley had a real shock. An enormous earthquake, measuring 6.4 on the Richter scale, hit Northridge, Los Angeles, at 9.30 a.m. Many buildings collapsed, and trees fell down, but amazingly there were few casualties. Rob King, a postman, was outside mending his car at the time. 'I didn't know what was happening,' he told me afterwards. 'I shouted to my brother. He was carrying a pot of tea. He dropped it as he ran outside.'

I spoke to several other inhabitants of Northridge. Hannah ...... was washing her ...... and didn't feel the quake at first. 'My ...... felt it first,' she said. 'He was ...... the cat.' Antonio Gonzales was ...... oranges when it started. 'My children ...... in the next field. They were really frightened, but they were OK.'

The next person I spoke to was called ...

Think about it!

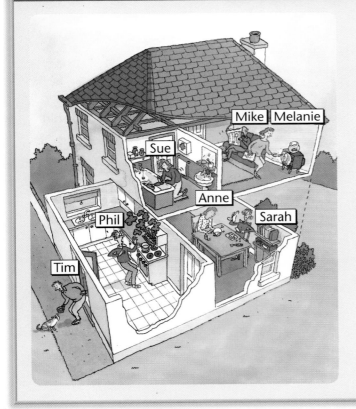

1 What were they doing when the fire started?

feed the cat   cook dinner   make a model
mend a bowl   ~~watch TV~~   clean the bathroom

a Mike and Melanie _were watching TV._

b Sarah ....

c Tim ....

d Anne ....

e Phil ....

f Sue ....

2 Read the example and underline the verbs.

Mike and Melanie were watching TV when the fire started.

a Which verb describes a continuous action?

b Which verb tells us about an event which interrupts a continuous action?

Choose and circle.

Easy   OK   Difficult

SCHOOL LIFE
PEOPLE AND PLACES
FREE TIME
ENTERTAINMENT

Vocabulary

1 **Look at the photos and read the texts. Which person is trying:**

a to save energy?   d to re-use rubbish in different ways?

b not to cause pollution?   e to recycle?

c not to harm animals?   f to protect forests?

1 I avoid materials which come from animals – like ivory, for example, which comes from elephants. I don't wear things made of fur, and I even avoid buying leather shoes. Wool is OK, though – the sheep don't get hurt!

4 I'm an artist, and I enjoy making things out of rubbish – like this model aeroplane, which I made from old aluminium cans. In fact, I hate throwing things away. I even keep my old woollen clothes and cotton handkerchiefs, and use them for cleaning.

I don't use my car for short journeys. I walk, or go by bike. It's better for my health, and it doesn't pollute the atmosphere. **2**

I'm careful not to waste electricity. For example, I always turn the lights off when I leave a room. And I don't have the TV on when I'm not watching it.

3 I only buy writing paper and envelopes made from recycled paper. And when I buy something made of wood, like a wooden table, I make sure it comes from a forest where they plant new trees.

6 I take my empty bottles, jars, and anything else made of glass to the recycling centre every week. I try not to buy plastic bottles because you can't recycle most kinds of plastic.

2 **Look at the pictures, and answer the questions.**

a What is each thing made of? Complete the labels with materials from Exercise 1.

b Think of other things at home and at school which are made of these materials.

c Which things can you recycle or re-use in a different way?

Word grammar

3 **Words for materials can be nouns or adjectives. Copy the table into your notebook and add as many more examples from this page as you can. Which two adjectives are different from their nouns?**

Noun	Adjective
you can't recycle <u>plastic</u>	<u>plastic</u> bottles
something made of <u>wood</u>	
	<u>woollen</u> jumpers

1 .... chopsticks

2 .... T-shirt

3 .... jumper

4 .... table

5 .... container

6 .... bottle

7 .... can

8 .... bag

Language focus

1 Read the questionnaire. Put a tick (✓) if it's the right thing to do, and a cross (✗) if it's the wrong thing to do.

HOW CAN WE TAKE CARE OF OUR ENVIRONMENT?

1 ....

✔ • use recycled paper

✗ • throw away paper bags

• use both sides of a piece of paper

• use cotton napkins, not paper ones

2 ....

• leave the lights on

• use re-chargeable batteries

• turn off the tap when you brush your teeth

• have showers instead of baths

3 ....

• travel by bicycle

• use strong chemicals for cleaning

4 ....

• re-use plastic bags and containers as many times as possible

• throw away empty bottles

• recycle empty aluminium cans

• avoid unnecessary food packaging

5 ....

• buy things made of ivory

• wear man-made fur instead of real fur

2 Choose a heading for each group and write it in the questionnaire.

Don't cause pollution   Don't create rubbish
Don't waste water or energy   Save trees
Protect endangered animals

FOCUS

should/shouldn't

● **Look at this sentence. Write two more examples using things you ticked in the questionnaire.**

We should use recycled paper.

● **Look at this sentence. Write two more examples using things you crossed in the questionnaire.**

We shouldn't throw away paper bags.

● **Complete these sentences with *should* or *shouldn't*.**

We can use .... to talk about what we think is the right thing to do.

We can use .... to talk about what we think is the wrong thing to do.

3 Using your answers to the questionnaire, say what we should or shouldn't do.

We shouldn't leave the lights on. We should turn the lights off when we're not using them.

4 Think about why we should or shouldn't do the things in the questionnaire. Explain your reasons.

We should use recycled paper.

If we use recycled paper, we'll save trees.

If we don't use recycled paper, a lot of trees will be destroyed.

Look!

If we <u>leave</u> the taps <u>on</u>, we'll waste water.

If we <u>don't turn</u> the taps <u>off</u>, we'll waste water.

5 What other things can we do to help the environment?

We should recycle paper. → *If we don't, we'll destroy forests.*

We shouldn't throw away things, we can re-use. → *If we do, we'll pollute the environment.*

Skills focus

Recycling the hard way

1 Look at the newspaper photos below. Then read and discuss the questions
in the table in pairs. Make notes of your ideas in the first column.

	your ideas	what the article says
a What's he eating? Name as many things as you can.		
b Do people usually eat these things?		
c Why is he eating them?		
d Where does he find them?		
e What do his family and friends think about him?		
f What do his neighbours think about him?		

2 Now read the article and complete the second
column of the table. Compare your ideas with
the answers from the article.
What was the same? What was different?

Look!

🇬🇧	rubbish	=	🇺🇸	garbage
🇬🇧	dustbin	=	🇺🇸	garbage can

Human dustbin eats rubbish!

Nature nut Frank Nichols has his own strange way of making America cleaner for our kids. He looks through garbage cans for garbage that can damage our environment – and he eats it!

"People think I'm crazy and maybe I am. But I'm trying to send a message to everybody," said Frank, 62. "I'm going to do it for as long as my stomach can take it."

Frank's one-man war begins shortly before sunrise every day, seven days a week, behind local supermarkets in Detroit, Michigan. He fills his mouth with plastic cups, paper plates, newspapers, aluminium foil, old milk cartons, and eats them. Frank says he has eaten nearly 30 tons of garbage in the last six months.

"I have my own personal garbage disposal system," said Frank, who also eats aluminium cans, old batteries and glass. He left a well-paid accountant's job so he could spend all his time cleaning up the town.

"I may be just a small drop in the ocean, but at least I'm trying."

Eccentric Frank has paid a terrible price for his beliefs. "My wife walked out a week after I told her how I was going to clean up the country. She called me a crackpot with bad breath," he explained.

Fearless Frank has also lost many of his close friends. People cross to the other side of the road when they see him coming. And he has stomach problems – bad stomach problems.

But Frank doesn't plan to stop fighting. In fact, he's hoping others will join him. "Together we can make a difference," he says.

3 Find these expressions in the article and answer the questions.

a "... paid a terrible price ..."

Did Frank pay any money? What was the 'price' he paid. Say where you found the answer.

b "Together we can make a difference."

Who are 'we'? How do you know?

c "... just a small drop in the ocean ..."

Is Frank talking about the sea? Does he think he is making a big difference?

4 In groups, discuss these questions. Give opinions and reasons, then share your ideas with the class.

a What do you think of Frank? Would you like to live next door to him? Why?/Why not?

b Is his method the best way of cleaning up the country? Why?/Why not?

c Can you suggest any other ways in which he could clean up the country?

5 In groups, make a poster to show the best ways of cleaning up the environment.

a Work together to write and correct the texts.

b Choose pictures and agree the layout.

c Display your poster for the rest of the class to see.

LOOKING AFTER the ENVIRONMENT

We should clean up our beaches. And we shouldn't dump any more rubbish in the sea.

GLASS GLAS
BROWN CLEA GLAS GREEN

We should use our cars less. If we don't, air pollution will get worse. We should travel by bike instead!

We should recycle glass bottles. We should avoid plastic bottles and containers.

Think about it!

1 Look at the pictures. Complete the labels with these words:

woollen ~~plastic~~ metal wooden

a

a plastic.. bottle.

c

a .... hat

b

a .... box

d

a .... knife

2 What is each of the things in Exercise 1 made of? Write the nouns.

a plastic.... b ....

c .... d ....

3 Write two more things we should do to help the environment.

We should save energy.

....

....

4 Write two more things we shouldn't do.

We shouldn't cause pollution.

....

....

Choose and circle.

Easy   OK   Difficult

Revision

Units 6–10

Stop and think!

- Do the exercises on pages 48–51. Start with section A, *'have to/ needn't'*.
- Look at the HELP screens if you need more practice.

A	*have to/needn't*	OK	HELP
B	Routines	OK	HELP
C	Present simple/ continuous	OK	HELP
D	Present passive	OK	HELP
E	Past continuous	OK	HELP

- Colour each letter when you can do the section.

A B C D E

Well done!

A
- Look at the Focus box on page 29.
- See the Look! box on page 31.
- Read item 4 of the Grammar Summary.

B
- Look at the Focus box on page 33.
- Do Workbook Unit 7 Exercise 4.
- Look back at Units 5–6 of *Brainwaves 2*.

C
- Look back at Units 8–9 of *Brainwaves 2*.
- Think about your own school day and compare it with Susan's.
- Read items 8–9 of the Grammar Summary in *Brainwaves 2*.

D
- Look at the Focus box on page 37.
- Do Workbook Unit 8 Exercise 4.
- Read item 6 of the Grammar Summary.

E
- Look at the Focus box on page 41.
- Do Workbook Unit 9 Exercises 3–4.
- Read item 7 of the Grammar Summary.

A *have to/needn't*

1 **Sally's got a new job at a burger bar. Complete the dialogue with *has/have to*, or *needn't*.**

Manager You will start tomorrow at 7.30.
Sally Do I .... buy a uniform?

Manager No, you .... buy one. We'll give you one tomorrow. But you .... wear it at all times when you are working.
Sally What about food. Do I .... pay for my own lunch?
Manager No, you're allowed one free meal every day you work. But you can't eat it in the main restaurant, that's for customers only. You .... go to the staff-room to eat.
Sally But I don't like burgers.
Manager That's OK. You .... eat them if you don't like them.

● B Routines

1 **Look at columns 1 and 2 of the table and write sentences. Follow the example.**

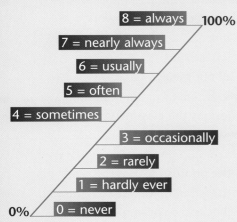

	① John	② Carol	③ Me	④ My partner
have shower before breakfast	7	1		
miss lunch	2	3		
do homework in class	8	4		
pretend to be ill on school days	5	0		
go to bed before midnight	8	6		

8 = always   100%
7 = nearly always
6 = usually
5 = often
4 = sometimes
3 = occasionally
2 = rarely
1 = hardly ever
0%   0 = never

John/shower
John nearly always has a shower before breakfast.

1 Carol/lunch
....

2 Carol/homework
....

3 John/ill
....

4 John/bed
....

5 Carol/ill
....

2 **Now complete column 3 of the table with information about yourself. Ask your partner questions using *How often ...?* and fill in column 4.**

3 **Write true sentences in your notebook about yourself and your partner using different adverbs from the list.**

● C Present simple/continuous

1 **Susan is making a video about a typical day in her life. Put the verbs in brackets into the present simple or continuous.**

Hi, my name's Susan Smith and this is my family. As you can see, we [1]..... (have) breakfast at the moment. We nearly always [2]..... (have) it at this time. Look, everyone [3]..... (smile) and happy. That is because I [4]..... (film) them – usually we [5]..... (not/talk) to each other in the mornings!

This is where I [6]..... (catch) the bus to school every day. It's the number 13, and it [7]..... (arrive) now. These two girls are my friends Tina and Becky. We all [8]..... (go) to the same school. Tina [9]..... (wear) a skirt today, which is unusual. She hardly ever [10]..... (wear) skirts.

I [11]..... (sit) on the bus now. It usually [12]..... (arrive) at school at about a quarter to nine. The bus driver [13]..... (shout) at the children at the back of the bus at the moment. He [14]..... (tell) them to sit down. The kids on the bus usually [15]..... (behave) very well. I [16]..... (not/know) what's wrong with them today.

This is my classroom. I always [17]..... (sit) at this desk, next to my friend Becky. Our teacher usually [18]..... (come) in at five past nine. She won't be very happy today because everyone [19]..... (make) a lot of noise. Oh, here she is! I [20]..... (have to) turn off the camera now. See you later!

D Present passive

1 In your notebooks, make sentences using the box below.

A meeting		given £5 pocket money a week.
Your personal details	am	interviewed in each issue.
A famous person	is	held in the editor's office every day.
These T-shirts		written and edited by students.
I	are	keyed into the computer.
The school magazine		decorated with fabric paints.

A meeting is held in the editor's office every day.

E Past continuous

1 **A car crashed into the Collins' house yesterday. Look at the picture and answer the questions below.**

What was the car passenger doing when the car crashed?

She was putting on make-up.

1 What was Mr Collins doing?
2 Who was working on the computer?
3 What was Sue doing?
4 Was Tim reading a newspaper?

2 **Write more questions and answers about the picture. Follow the example.**

the twins/sunbathe?

Were the twins sunbathing?

No, they weren't. They were playing basketball.

1 Mrs Collins and Mrs King/ eating?
2 Uncle Ben/mend car?
3 Simon/have bath?
4 dog/eat?

2 Rewrite these sentences using the passive and *by*.

Carole makes the models.

The models *are made by Carole.*

1 The teacher corrects our homework.
   Our homework ....
   ....
2 Dad cooks all our meals.
   All our meals ....
3 Samantha designs the class newspaper.
   The class newspaper ....
   ....
4 Terry takes the photos.
   The photos ....
5 The editor checks the spelling.
   The spelling ....

Reading and writing

1 Read Sam's description of his hobby.

My hobby is playing chess – the greatest game in the world. My mum taught me how to play when I was seven years old. She beat me every time for the first year. But then, on my eighth birthday, I won for the first time. I nearly always beat her now.

It takes about a day to learn the rules. But if you want to be good, you have to practise for years. You don't need much to play chess – just a chess set and someone to play with. Chess sets can be quite cheap, or incredibly expensive. Some people collect chess sets as a hobby, but I prefer to play.

There is a chess club in our school. We meet every week to play each other. I am the best player in the club, and the captain of the school chess team. This year we won the All England Schools' Championship, and I had to go up on stage in front of the whole school to collect the trophy.

I'm saving up my money to buy a chess computer. They are very expensive, but also very good for practice. That way I'll always have someone to play with. One day I want to be the world chess champion.

2 True or False?

1 Sam's Mum never beats him at chess.   ....
2 You have to spend a lot of money for a chess set. ....
3 Sam doesn't collect chess sets.   ....
4 Sam's school has a very good chess team.   ....
5 Sam has got a chess computer.   ....

3 Make notes about your hobby.

- when you started
- why you like it
- what you need
- what you did
- what you want to do

4 Write about your hobby using your notes.

Project idea

- Find some people in the class with the same hobby as you.
- Find out about the history of your hobby.
- Collect photographs.
- Make a 'hobby wall chart', giving people information about your hobby.

SCHOOL LIFE
PEOPLE AND PLACES
FREE TIME
ENTERTAINMENT

Vocabulary

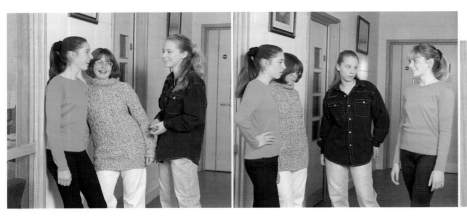

1 Look at the photos and describe what is happening in each one.

a Describe the people.

b What do you think they are doing and saying?

c How do you think they are feeling?

2 Read the letter. Which people in the photo can you name?

Dear Sue,

Joanna, a girl in my class, copies everything I do. Last week, I had a haircut, so she went and had exactly the same haircut the next day. Two days ago, I went to school wearing a new T-shirt, which everyone liked. Two days later, she came to school wearing an identical T-shirt. It's really beginning to annoy me! Everyone at school calls us 'the twins'.

My mum says she's probably jealous of me, but I don't know what to do about it. Please can you help me?

Yours,

Natalie

3 Read the list of adjectives.

popular   pessimistic   embarrassed   optimistic   nervous   insecure   excited   worried   jealous   self-conscious   confident   depressed   moody

a Use the glossary to check or find out the meaning of the words.

b Which adjectives in the list can you use to describe the people in the photos?

c Are the adjectives positive or negative? Copy and complete these diagrams.

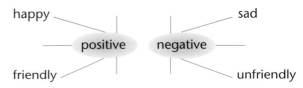

happy —————— sad

friendly —— positive   negative —— unfriendly

4 Imagine you are in the following situations. Talk in pairs about how you feel.

a You're wearing something new.

b You get home late.

c You tell a lie, and somebody finds out.

d You can't finish your homework on time.

e Your best friend ignores you.

Glossary

People who are **confident** feel that they can deal with situations, so they don't worry about them very much.

If you are **depressed**, you are sad and feel that you cannot enjoy anything.

People get **embarrassed** when something happens which makes them feel shy, ashamed, or guilty. Their face sometimes goes red.

If you are **excited**, you are so happy that you cannot relax. You feel full of energy.

People who are **insecure** feel unsure of themselves and their abilities. They don't think other people will like or respect them.

If you are **jealous**, you want to have or do the same things as somebody else. You feel that it's unfair if you can't.

A **moody** person gets sad or angry very quickly, and sometimes for no obvious reason.

Someone who feels **nervous** is worried about what will happen.

Someone who is **optimistic** is hopeful about the future, and believes that things will happen in the best possible way.

Someone who is **pessimistic** is not hopeful about the future, and believes that things will happen in the worst possible way.

Someone who is **popular** is liked by lots of people.

Someone who is **self-conscious** is shy, and doesn't feel comfortable, especially when other people are looking at them.

Some who is **worried** is unhappy because they keep thinking about problems, or about unpleasant things that might happen in the future.

Language focus

A radio phone-in

Dear Sue

I'm worried about my best friend. Something is making him sad, but he won't tell me what it is. Last year, he was always happy and good fun to be with, but now he's really moody and pessimistic. He wants to spend a lot of time on his own, but before he was really popular and friendly. When I ask him if he's got a problem, he gets angry and won't talk to me. I feel as if I don't know him any more. What's your advice? What do you think I should do?

John

1 🎧 ❶ **Natalie sent her letter to a radio programme for teenagers. Listen to the first part of the programme. What does Sue Wallace do?**

2 **What advice have you got for Natalie? Discuss it in pairs or groups and write your ideas.**

We think she should tell the girl to stop copying her.

3 🎧 ❷ **Listen to what Sue says to Natalie. Did you have the same advice?**

4 **Listen again and complete Sue's advice in your notebook.**

If I were you, I would ¹...... her for the compliment. Then maybe I'd ²...... that a different colour would look better on her. Look, Natalie, I'm sure it's just a temporary situation – she'll stop copying you soon. If I were you, I wouldn't ³...... about it too much.

5 **Read John's letter and answer the questions.**

a What is his problem?

b What two expressions does he use to ask for advice?

c Can you think of any advice to give him? Make notes.

6 **In pairs, role-play Jack Powell and Sue Wallace.**

Jack Introduce Sue and read the letter from John.

Sue Give advice and make suggestions. Use your notes from Exercise 5c.

7 **Now work in different pairs. Look at these situations and give each other advice. You can also invent other situations if you want.**

a Your friend keeps copying your homework.

b You don't get enough pocket money.

c Your parents make you come home by 6.30 at night.

d You are very shy and can't make friends.

FOCUS | ON AIR

If I were you ...

● **We can give advice or make a suggestion with this form:**

If I were you ..., I would/ wouldn't ...

● **Write examples of the form from Exercise 4. Then answer the questions.**

a What is the short form of *I would ...*?

b Sue says *If I were you, ...* because:

she has the same problem as Natalie ☐

she is imagining herself in Natalie's position ☐

she wants to be in Natalie's position ☐

● **Other ways of giving advice:**

I think you should listen to people more.
I don't think you should worry.
How about helping with the housework sometimes?
Why don't you buy her a present?

● Skills focus

Odd one out

1 Look at the headings for the letters. What
   problem do you think each letter will be about?

① Odd one out

Dear Sue,

I am 15 and have lots of friends, but I am still miserable. The problem is that they all look great and get lots of attention, but I get none. No one takes any notice of me. My best friend, Gina, is beautiful and always looks fantastic whatever she wears, and when I go out with her I feel really ugly.

I like all my friends, but what can I do to be more like them? Please give me some advice.

Anxious,
Dublin

② Spider terror

Dear Sue,

I know lots of people are scared of spiders, but I only have to see one and I start to shake and go hot and cold. In a Biology lesson last week, the teacher showed us a picture of a spider and I fainted. My teacher said it was a panic attack. Everyone thinks I'm silly to be like this, but I can't help it. I don't want to be this way. Please let me talk about it because no one understands how I feel.

What should I do?

Scared, 14
Newcastle

2 Read the letters quickly.

   a Were your ideas similar?
   b Which problem is about:
      not having control over a situation? ☐
      self-confidence? ☐
      fears? ☐

3 Read each letter again and make notes in the table.

	Letter 1	Letter 2	Letter 3
Personal information	age 15 from Dublin		
Problem			
Example of the problem			
Feelings			
Questions			

③

Homework misery

Dear Sue,

My life is awful this year because of too much homework. I didn't get too much at the beginning of the year, which was great because I had time to be with my friends, play football, listen to music and go to different places. But things changed really quickly. These days I hardly have enough time in the evening to finish all my work. At the end of the week I am tired, depressed and bored. What use is homework anyway?

Overworked, 14
Brighton

4 **Read these two replies to *Spider terror*. Which one do you think is better and why?**

a Well, you are being silly, aren't you? Spiders aren't dangerous, so why are you frightened? If I were you, I would just turn away when there's a spider. The spider won't hurt you. Stop being so nervous!

b I don't think you're being silly. Phobias are very serious and it's wrong of people to make fun of you. If you ask, you'll find that most people are afraid of something – the dark, snakes, flying. If I were you, I'd try to get more information about your problem. Try reading *Say Goodbye to Your Fears and Phobias* by Dr Robert Jones.

5 **What advice would you give to the writers of the other letters?**

a Choose *Anxious of Dublin*, or *Overworked of Brighton*. Make a list of your advice.

b Write a reply using *If I were you …* and phrases from the focus box.

c Read your letter to the class. Do they agree or disagree with your advice?

I agree. I think that's good advice.

I don't agree. I don't think he / she should do that.

Think about it!

1 **Label the pictures with these adjectives:**

embarrassed   excited   ~~nervous~~   depressed

nervous

....

....

....

2 **Complete the sentences in your own words.**

a I feel embarrassed when ....

b I get excited when ....

c I get nervous when ....

d I feel depressed when ....

3 **Rewrite the sentences. Say the same thing in a different way.**

a I think you should talk to her.

   If I were you, I'd talk to her.

b How about writing a letter to him?

   ....

c If I were you, I'd buy a new bike.

   ....

d I don't think you should buy that CD.

   ....

e If I were you, I wouldn't go.

   ....

Choose and circle.

Easy   OK   Difficult

SCHOOL LIFE
PEOPLE AND PLACES
FREE TIME
ENTERTAINMENT

● Vocabulary

1 **Do you believe everything you hear or read? Try to remember an example of:**

a something you believed which turned out not be true.

b something you didn't believe which turned out to be true.

2 **Read these expressions.**

a Which three mean you believe someone? Which five mean you don't believe someone? Which two mean you aren't sure?

a It can't be true.

b It must be true.

c It could be true.

d It sounds OK to me.

e You're having me on.

f I don't believe that.

g It sounds possible.

h No, that's impossible.

i Yes, I believe that.

j You're making it up.

b Look at the five expressions of disbelief. Are some of them stronger than others? Which ones?

c 🖭 ❶ Listen and repeat all the expressions.

3 **Read these eight pieces of information. Use the pictures to help you understand. Do you think they are all true?**

4 **Which information do you believe?**

a Discuss the information in pairs or groups. Use expressions from Exercise 2.

> The one about the youngest king can't be true.

> I don't agree. It sounds possible to me.

b Make a note of your decisions. Put a tick (✓) for the ones you believe, a cross (✗) for the ones you don't believe, and a question mark (?) if you aren't sure.

c Compare your decisions with other pairs or groups, and explain your reasons. Which ones do you agree about?

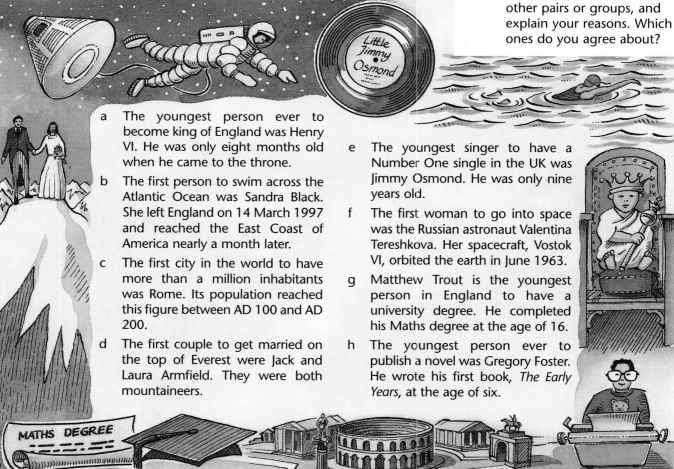

a The youngest person ever to become king of England was Henry VI. He was only eight months old when he came to the throne.

b The first person to swim across the Atlantic Ocean was Sandra Black. She left England on 14 March 1997 and reached the East Coast of America nearly a month later.

c The first city in the world to have more than a million inhabitants was Rome. Its population reached this figure between AD 100 and AD 200.

d The first couple to get married on the top of Everest were Jack and Laura Armfield. They were both mountaineers.

e The youngest singer to have a Number One single in the UK was Jimmy Osmond. He was only nine years old.

f The first woman to go into space was the Russian astronaut Valentina Tereshkova. Her spacecraft, Vostok VI, orbited the earth in June 1963.

g Matthew Trout is the youngest person in England to have a university degree. He completed his Maths degree at the age of 16.

h The youngest person ever to publish a novel was Gregory Foster. He wrote his first book, *The Early Years*, at the age of six.

MATHS DEGREE

● Language focus

Golden boy Marcus

GOLDEN BOY MARCUS – ALMOST AT THE TOP

Super-successful Marcus Samson has done it all – and he's still only 18. He set up his own computer games company two years ago, and has already become a millionaire.

He not only has a talent for making money, but he has succeeded in everything else he has tried. 'I've done everything, I've been everywhere, I've lived life to the full,' he says.

His list of achievements is truly amazing. In his short life he has already:

● joined the list of The 200 Richest People in Britain, with £2.7 million in the bank.

● travelled to almost every country in the world. 'America is my favourite,' he says. 'I haven't been to Australia yet, but I plan to go there next month.'

● learned five languages. 'Japanese is an interesting language, but I like Norwegian best,' he says.

● married one of the most beautiful girls in the world, top fashion model Fay Waif.

1 Look at the photo and describe the people. What do you think the article is about? What kind of people do you think they are?

2 Read the newspaper article.

a How did Marcus become rich?

b What does he say about himself?

c How is Marcus connected with these things or people?

200 richest people *He is on the list of the 200 Richest People in Britain.*

America Norwegian Fay Waif

Present perfect

● **Use the present perfect for talking about experiences and achievements.**

I've done everything, I've been everywhere.

● **The present perfect tense is formed from the present of the verb *have* and a past participle. Look at these examples.**

I've lived life to the full.

He has succeeded in everything else he has tried.

I haven't been to Australia yet.

3 Here are some more things Marcus says he has done. Make sentences.

a set / world record / bungee-jumping
   He's set the world record for bungee-jumping.

b buy / luxury houses / Hawaii, Thailand, and the South of France

c cross / Atlantic Ocean / hot-air balloon

d make / hit record

e sign / contract / Warner Brothers film studios

4 Imagine you are Marcus. Invent some more achievements.

I've played football at Wembley.

5 Work with a partner and make notes.

a Talk about things you have done in your life.
   I've been to England.

b Talk about things you haven't done, but would like to.
   I haven't used a computer yet, but I'd like to.

● Skills focus

Truth or fiction?

1   **Look at the photo.**

a   Who or what do you think this TV show is about?

b   Find these people in the picture and number them:

Ben Yates, friend ☐

Fay Waif, fashion model ☐

Marcus Samson, 'golden boy' ☐

Molly Jones, neighbour ☐

Rachel Krantz, TV presenter ☐

2   **Make a list of everything Marcus says he has done.**

a   First, try to remember. Use these words to remind yourself.

millionaire	travel	languages
marry	bungee-jumping	luxury houses
hot-air balloon	record	film studios

He's already become a millionaire.

He's travelled …

b   Now look back at Language focus and check your list.

c   Do you believe that Marcus has done all of these things?

3   📻 **❷ Listen to the first part of the TV show.**

a   Use your list from Exercise 2a. Tick (✓) the things Marcus really has done, cross (✗) the things he hasn't.

He's already become a millionaire.   ✗

b   It's easier to follow a dialogue if you listen out for key words. Use the list in Exercise 2a to help you decide which words to listen for.

4   **Use your answers from Exercise 3 to talk about what Marcus has or hasn't done.**

He hasn't become a millionaire. He's only got £27 in his bank account.

5 Look at this photo from another part of the TV show. What do you think this man says has happened?

6 🔊 ❸ **Listen and check your answers to Exercise 5. Then listen again and tick (✓) Mike's experiences.**

a lost his hat ☐
b visited Mars and Venus ☐
c seen Elvis Presley ☐
d travelled back in time ☐
e been a scientific experiment ☐
f drunk liquids that don't exist on earth ☐
g eaten chicken and rice ☐
h talked Chinese ☐
i seen right through his body ☐

7 Look at the experiences in Exercise 6 that you didn't tick. Correct the statements.

He's lost his coat and shoes.

8 Do you believe Mike's story? Why? Why not?

9 Work in groups of 3 or 4. Write about an experience you have had. Then write about an imaginary experience.

Student A: Tell the rest of the group about your experiences. They must decide which one is true and which one is a lie.

Students B, C, D: Listen to the speaker and try to decide which experience is true and which one is false. Use the phrases you learned in Vocabulary.

Think about it!

1 Write two more expressions of belief, and two more of disbelief.

Yes, I believe that.

....

....

No, I don't believe that.

....

....

2 Write true sentences about yourself. Use the present perfect, positive or negative.

a visit/England

I've visited England./I haven't visited England.

b eat/Indian food

....

c make/a record

....

d buy/a CD

....

e write/a letter today

....

3 Write three more things you have done, and three more you haven't done.

I have ....

....

....

I haven't ....

....

....

Choose and circle.

Easy   OK   Difficult

Vocabulary

SCHOOL LIFE
PEOPLE AND PLACES
FREE TIME
ENTERTAINMENT

1 **Look at the picture. The actions and objects are typical dream images. Have you ever had dreams like these?**

2 **Which of these dream images can you see in the picture?**

climbing	swimming	mountain
crashing	walking	plane
driving	corridor	room
drowning	dark	vehicle
falling	door	water
flying	flood	
running away	flowers	

I can see a mountain.

There's someone running down a corridor.

3 **Describe the dreams in the picture using these words.**

a frightening

b strange

c pleasant

d unpleasant

Falling off a mountain is frightening.

4 **Many people believe that dream symbols have a meaning. Read the text and answer the questions.**

a What does a mountain symbolize?

b What does falling mean in a dream?

c What does falling off a mountain mean?

A mountain means a problem or difficulty. Falling is associated with fear, worry, and anxiety. It means that you are afraid that you will fail. So falling off a mountain symbolizes a problem you do not think you can solve.

5 **What do you think the other dream images in Exercise 2 mean? Discuss them with a partner, then tell the class.**

Word grammar

6 **Read the example. Which of these words can you use to replace the underlined word in the example?**

water   see   frightening

Falling symbolizes anxiety.

7 **Think about your answer to Exercise 6. What part of speech is *falling* in the example?**

Language focus

Dream on

We all dream every night. We don't remember most of our dreams, but sometimes a particular dream stays in our minds for days, or maybe even weeks. Have you ever had a nightmare you can't forget? Have you ever dreamt about the same thing night after night?

Mandy: "I've often dreamt that someone is chasing me. It's a recurring dream. Last time I had it, I was going to school because we had a test that day. As I went inside the school, something followed me in. I knew it was something horrible, so I started running down the corridor. I ran and ran, but it was still there. Suddenly I saw a light at the end of the corridor. Then I woke up. The dream was really frightening."

Kazim: "Last week, I dreamt I was flying to Ankara to see my cousin. Then, suddenly the plane began to fall from the sky. I saw the earth getting nearer and nearer. I closed my eyes and screamed. Then I woke up. What a nightmare!"

1 **Read the magazine article about dreams. Then answer the questions.**

   a Who has dreamt about being chased?

   b Who has had a recurring dream?

   c Who had a nightmare about a plane crash?

2 ▦❶ **Read and answer the questions. Then listen to the first part of an expert talking about the meaning of dreams and compare your ideas.**

   a What do you think Mandy's dream means?

   b What do you think Kazim's dream means?

3 ▦❷ **Listen to the second part of the tape. What does the expert say about these other dream symbols?**

   a fire

   b climbing

   c water

4 **Find out about different types of dreams your partner has had. Tell your partner about your own dreams. Try to explain the meaning of each other's dreams.**

FOCUS

Present perfect and past simple

● **Study the examples. Then complete sentences a and b below with these words:**

present   past simple perfect

<u>Have</u> you ever <u>had</u> a nightmare?
   No, I <u>haven't</u>.

<u>Have</u> you ever <u>dreamt</u> about a plane crash?
   Yes, I <u>have</u>. A few nights ago, I <u>dreamt</u> that I was flying across the sea …

   a To ask and answer about an experience some time in the past we use the ....
      ....

   b To describe something that happened in the past we use the ....

● **Ask and answer about the dreams in Vocabulary.**

Have you ever dreamt that you were falling?
   No, I haven't. / Yes, I have. I dreamt …

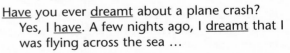

● **Skills focus**

A Book of Dreams

Octopus's Garden

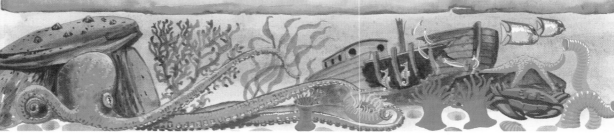

I'd like to be under the sea
In an octopus's garden in the shade
He'd let us in, know where we've been
In his octopus's garden in the shade
I'd ask my friends to come and see
An octopus's garden with me

I'd like to be under the sea
In an octopus's garden in the shade

We would be warm before the storm
In our little hideaway beneath the waves
Resting our head on the sea bed
In an octopus's garden near a cave
We would sing and dance around
Because we know we can't be found

I'd like to be under the sea
In an octopus's garden in the shade

We would shout and swim about
The coral that lies beneath the waves
Oh what joy for every girl and boy
Knowing they're happy and they're safe
We would be so happy, you and me
No one there to tell us what to do

I'd like to be under the sea
In an octopus's garden in the shade

1 Read the texts below. Is it good to have these kinds of dream? Why?/Why not?

DAYDREAMING _____

We don't only dream at night – we also dream during the day. We daydream when we're sitting on the bus, sitting at our desks, or waiting for someone to arrive. When we daydream, we make up stories about ourselves, or imagine ourselves in a different place or situation. We think about where we'd really like to be, and what we'd like to be doing.

DREAMS FOR THE FUTURE _____

Do you have dreams about the future? Do you think about what you would like to be or do when you're older? Most people do. But most people's dreams for the future change as they get older. Have your dreams always been the same, or have they changed?

2 Look at the *Book of dreams.* Which part is a song about a daydream? Which part is about dreams for the future? Which part describes a night-time dream?

3 Write about your dreams for the future. Use the outlines to help you.

When I was little, I ..... I've changed my mind many times since then.
First, I ..... and then ......
Now, I .....

OR

Ever since I was little, I have always wanted ....., because .....

4 Write about your daydreams. Use these questions to help you.

a What do you like to daydream about?

b If you didn't have to be here, where would you like to be?

c Who would you be? What would you do?

d What's the picture in your mind?

5 🎹 ❸ Read and listen to *Octopus's Garden.*

a Is this the kind of thing you daydream about? Is it a nice daydream?

b Listen again and sing.

6 Work in groups. Make your own book of dreams.

a Include texts, songs, or poems about daydreams, night-time dreams, and dreams for the future.

b Add appropriate photos and illustrations.

c Display your work for other groups to see.

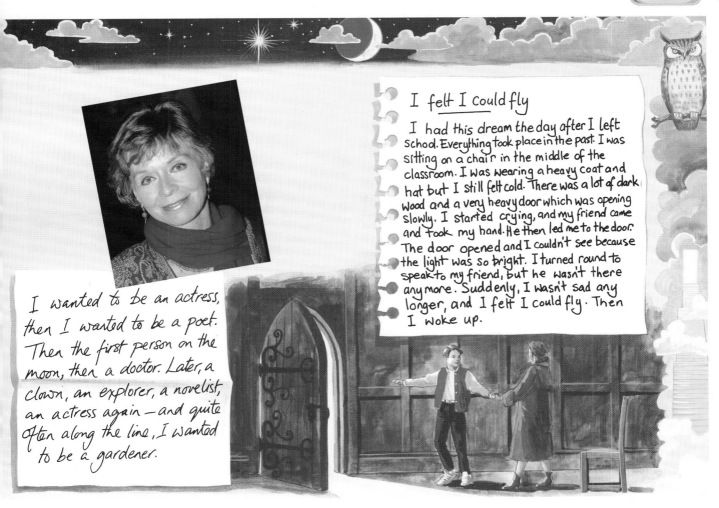

I wanted to be an actress, then I wanted to be a poet. Then the first person on the moon, then a doctor. Later, a clown, an explorer, a novelist, an actress again — and quite often along the line, I wanted to be a gardener.

I felt I could fly

I had this dream the day after I left school. Everything took place in the past. I was sitting on a chair in the middle of the classroom. I was wearing a heavy coat and hat but I still felt cold. There was a lot of dark wood and a very heavy door which was opening slowly. I started crying, and my friend came and took my hand. He then led me to the door. The door opened and I couldn't see because the light was so bright. I turned round to speak to my friend, but he wasn't there any more. Suddenly, I wasn't sad any longer, and I felt I could fly. Then I woke up.

Think about it!

1 Complete the sentences with the *-ing* form of these verbs:

fly   ~~climb~~   swim   fall   run away   drive

a There's a man climbing a mountain.

b There's a plane .... over some trees.

c There's a woman .... a vehicle.

d There's a man .... into a river.

e There's a woman .... in the sea.

f There's a child .... from a flood.

2 Match these pictures with the sentences from Exercise 1.

1 C.

2 .....

3 .....

4 .....

5 .....

6 .....

3 Answer the questions.

a Have you ever dreamt about any of the things in Exercises 1 and 2?

....

b When did you last have a dream?

....

c Describe your last dream.

....

....

Choose and circle.

Easy   OK   Difficult

SCHOOL LIFE
PEOPLE AND PLACES
FREE TIME
ENTERTAINMENT

● Vocabulary

1 aerobics

2 snowboarding

3 cycling

4 weight-training

5 swimming

6 rock-climbing

7 windsurfing

8 martial arts

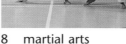

9 yoga

1 Look at the photos and answer the questions.

a Where are the people?

b What are they doing?

c Have you ever done any of these activities? What about other keep-fit activities?

d Did you enjoy them? Why?/Why not?

2 Read about these people's favourite ways to keep fit.

a Which activity is each person talking about?

b Which words help you to work out the answers?

1 My favourite keep-fit activity is ..... A **guy** I met on holiday last summer encouraged me to **have a go at it**. It was difficult at first, but now I'm starting to **get the hang of it**. And it's much more fun than **just sitting around** on the beach.

2 I'm **really into** ..... If you like music and you enjoy dancing, it's the perfect way to get fit. But you should start with a class for beginners. Don't **pick** a class which is only for **super-fit** people – you won't be able to do it.

3 I love the winter, because it means I can go ..... I just love the fresh air and the scenery, but the best thing about it is the speed! The first time I tried it, I found it really **scary**. But as soon as I got to the bottom of the mountain, **I couldn't wait to** do it again!

3 🔊 **①** **Listen and check your answers to Exercise 2a.**

4 Look at the texts again. The expressions in bold are all colloquial (spoken, everyday language).

a Match them to their explanations below.

1 very fit   *super-fit*

2 try it   ......

3 really keen on   ......

4 frightening   ......

5 not doing very much   ......

6 boy (or man)   ......

7 choose   ......

8 immediately wanted to   ......

9 be able to do it   ......

b When is it a good idea to use colloquial expressions? Tick (✓) or cross (✗).

in a letter to your penfriend   ☐

in an exam   ☐

when you are talking to a friend   ☐

when you are talking to an adult you've just met   ☐

5 Tell your classmates about other good ways to keep fit. They can be activities from this page or any other activities you know.

I'm really into …

I'd really like to have a go at …

● Language focus

Harry and Bill

1 **Look at the pictures and describe the two men.**

2 🎙️ ❷ **Listen to Harry and Bill and write their names on the correct picture of how they look now.**

....

....

3 **Listen again. Tick (✓) the correct column.**

Who used to:	Harry	Bill
a take a lot of exercise?	☐	☐
b be fat?	☐	☐
c play football?	☐	☐
d be an accountant?	☐	☐
e go to the gym?	☐	☐
f be very fit?	☐	☐
g eat a much better diet?	☐	☐
h eat crisps, chocolate, and chips?	☐	☐

FOCUS

used to

● **Answer these questions.**

  a Is Harry an accountant now?

  b Was he an accountant in the past?

  c What's his job now?

● **We use *used to* to talk about things we did regularly in the past but don't do any more. Complete these sentences.**

  Harry .... be an accountant, but now he .... a windsurfing instructor.

● **Study the examples to find out how we make questions and negative sentences with *used to*.**

  Did he use to go to the gym?
    No, he didn't. He didn't use to do any exercise at all.
  Did he use to be unhealthy?
    Yes, he did.

4 **Complete this paragraph about Harry with *used to* or *didn't use to*.**

I ¹..... be very unfit. I ²..... eat a lot of crisps, chocolate, and chips. I ³..... eat healthy food at all. But one day, I looked in the mirror and saw a fat, unhealthy man. I started going to the gym, and eating salads, chicken, and fruit. I changed my job, too. I ⁴..... be an accountant, but now I'm a windsurfing instructor.

5 **Now write a paragraph about Bill. Use the information from Exercise 3.**

6 **Think of some things you used to do. Tell your partner about them, then ask questions.**

I used to fall off my bike, but I can ride it now. Did you use to fall off your bike, too?

Skills focus

An interview with Will Murphy

Will Murphy is the new thirteen-year-old star of *Blades*. Will plays the part of Jem, Laurie's son, in the weekly TV drama about rollerblading.

1 **You're going to read an interview with Will Murphy. What questions would you ask if you were the interviewer? In pairs, make a list.**

2 **Read the actual questions from the interview. Are any of them the same as the ones on your list?**

a Did you use to be a fan of *Blades* before you got the part?

b Do you have to be super-fit to play the part?

c Have you been in any other TV shows or films?

d How did you feel when you got the part?

e How did you get the part in *Blades*?

f How do you get on with the other actors?

g What do you think you'll do next?

h When did you first start rollerblading?

3 **Read Will's answers and match them to the questions in Exercise 2.**

e It was simple, really. I saw an advert in the newspaper and went along for an audition. I didn't expect to get the part, at all.

☐ I was amazed. They phoned me the day after the audition to tell me the good news. I couldn't believe it. I think I just stood there with my mouth open, not speaking for ages.

☐ No. In fact, I didn't use to watch it all. It used to be on quite late – around 11.00 p.m. I think. I was usually in bed by that time.

☐ Yes, I suppose it helps if you're fit. I mean, I was really into rollerblading anyway, before I even thought about acting. And rollerblading's pretty good exercise – it keeps me in good condition, physically.

☐ I started about three years ago. I got a pair of rollerblades for my birthday – and I couldn't wait to get outside and have a go! It was difficult at first, but I soon got the hang of it.

☐ Well, I was in a film once, when I was really young – about three. I didn't have to say much – I just had to cry a lot. Until recently, my friends used to make fun of that. But now I've got a proper part in a really good TV show, they're all jealous.

☐ I get on fine with them. They're all older than me, but they treat me really well. And Roxanne, who plays my mum Laurie in the show, is wonderful. She looks after me – like a real mother!

☐ Next? It's difficult to say. I'd like to be in *Blades* for a few more years. Then, when I'm older, I'd like to make films. Maybe I'll move to Hollywood – who knows?

Pronunciation

4 🎧 ❸ **Listen to the questions in the correct order.**

a Check your answers to Exercise 3.

b Listen again and underline the stressed words in each question.

   <u>How</u> did you get the <u>part</u> in <u>Blades</u>?

c Usually, we stress words which carry the main information. Look at your answer to b again. Are all the underlined words important?

5 **In pairs, role-play an interview with Will Murphy.**

Student A: Ask questions from the list you prepared in Exercise 1. Try to stress the important words. Make a note of Student B's answers.

Student B: Use your imagination to invent the answers.

Walking on Sunshine

I used to think maybe you loved me. Now, baby, I'm sure
And I just can't wait till the day when you knock on my door
Now every time I go for the mailbox, I gotta hold myself down
Because I just can't wait till you write me you're coming around

I'm walking on sunshine, I'm walking on sunshine
I'm walking on sunshine, and it's time to feel good
It's time to feel good

I used to think maybe you loved me. Now I know that it's true
But I don't want to spend my whole life just waiting for you
Now, I don't want you back for the weekend, not back for a day
I said baby, I just want you back, and I want you to stay

I'm walking on sunshine, I'm walking on sunshine
I'm walking on sunshine, and it's time to feel good
It's time to feel good

6 **Look at the picture. What kind of song do you think this is?**

fast slow sad happy exciting relaxing

7 **When do you like to sing? When you're:**

happy sad relaxed excited worried

8 🎵 ④ **Read and listen to the song. Then answer the questions.**

a What did she use to think?

b How does she feel now?

c What does she want to happen in the future?

9 **Now listen and sing!**

Think about it!

1 **Match the pictures with the keep-fit activities.**

snow-boarding ..c..   swimming .....

windsurfing   .....   yoga   .....

judo   .....

2 **Complete the text in your own words.**

When I was five years old, I used to ....
....
....

I also used to ....
....

I didn't use to ....
....

3 **Write five more questions to ask your partner about when he or she was five years old.**

a *Did you use to go to school?*

b ....

c ....

d ....

e ....

f ....

Choose and circle.

Easy   OK   Difficult

SCHOOL LIFE
PEOPLE AND PLACES
FREE TIME
ENTERTAINMENT

🎧 Vocabulary

1 **Look at these teenagers. They're all about to take exams!**

a How do you think they feel?

b Do you ever feel the same way before an exam?

c Do you ever feel the same way in other situations?

2 **Talk about the teenagers in the pictures. Use these expressions.**

get — upset / anxious / nervous / tired

get — fit / organized

get — to sleep / into a panic

get — enough sleep / plenty of vitamins / some exercise

be — calm / confident

She's getting some exercise.
He can't get to sleep.

3 **Read the questionnaire.**

a Match the underlined phrases with the pictures (a–i).

b Which words helped you to match the phrases and pictures? Did you learn any new words while you were doing it?

c Which phrases can you say in a different way using expressions from Exercise 2?

4 **Answer the questionnaire.**

REVISION TIME

1 Do you get anxious before exams? How does your anxiety show? Do you:

a <u>bite your nails</u>? ☐

b bite your lips? ☐

c <u>chew your pencil</u>? ☐

d play with your hair? ☐

2 During your revision period do you:

a <u>sometimes cry</u>? ☐

b feel tense? ☐

c feel very tired? ☐

d <u>find you can't sleep</u>? ☐

e lack energy? ☐

f <u>remain calm</u>? ☐

3 How do you plan your revision?

a I don't. I just revise a bit of this, then revise a bit of that. ☐

b I revise one subject, then the next subject, and so on. ☐

c I <u>make a timetable</u> so that I do a little revision of two or three subjects each evening. ☐

4 In the lead-up to the exams, do you:

a <u>take regular exercise</u>? ☐

b <u>eat a balanced diet?</u> ☐

c go to bed late? ☐

d <u>drink a lot of fizzy drinks</u>, tea, or coffee? ☐

e give up your social life? ☐

Now compare answers with your classmates.

● Language focus

Five steps to relieving exam stress

1 Make a revision timetable. A clear timetable will help you to be more organized.

2 Eat a balanced diet. Lack of vitamins increases stress and makes the body weak.

3 Don't revise too late at night. Too much mental work will keep you awake, and make you sleepy the next day. Avoid tea, coffee, or fizzy drinks in the evening, too.

4 Get plenty of exercise. It will help you to relax.

5 Talk to people about your worries. Bottling up your emotions can cause a lot of stress.

1 Read the title of the article. Who do you think the article is written for?

2 Read the article. Match each of the five steps to the appropriate picture.

3 Look at pictures 1–5 below and read the captions. What should each person do, according to the article?

1 She can't relax.
She should get more exercise.

2 He's disorganized. ▶

◀3 She's suffering from a lot of stress.

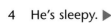
4 He's sleepy. ▶

◀5 He feels weak.

4 Look at these comments about the first girl in the pictures. Do you agree with them?

If she got more exercise, she would be able to relax.

She'd feel healthier if she went jogging every day.

FOCUS

The second conditional

● **Look at the example. Then answer the questions.**

If she got more exercise, she would be able to relax.

a Does she get a lot of exercise?
b Can she relax?

● **We can use the second conditional to talk about what would happen if the situation was different.**

● **A second conditional sentence has two parts.**

If + past form, *would* + base form

● **We can change the order of the parts.**

She'd feel healthier if she went jogging every day.

5 Look at your answers to Exercise 3 again. Talk about the people using the second conditional.

If he ate a balanced diet, he wouldn't feel weak.

6 Do you agree with everything the article says? Have you got any other ideas of your own? Discuss them in pairs.

I don't agree with number 4 in the article. If I did a lot of exercise before an exam, I'd be exhausted. I think it's better to get plenty of rest.

● Skills focus

Improve your revision techniques

1 Look at the pictures. Which one are you more like, the swot or the crammer?

2 You are going to listen to *Exam Tips,* a radio programme which gives advice about exams. What do you think it will suggest?

3 📼 ❶ Read the list of advice. Then listen and tick (✓) the advice mentioned in the programme.

Don't drink too much caffeine. ☐

Revise as you go along. ☐

Eat a balanced diet. ☐

Find a quiet place to study. ☐

Don't leave it to the last minute. ☐

Make a revision timetable. ☐

Go to bed early. ☐

Cut down on your social life. ☐

Don't stay in every evening. ☐

Keep calm and don't worry. ☐

4 What do you think of the presenter's ideas? Do you think they are practical? What would you suggest?

5 Read the text about ways to help you remember information. Match the techniques with pictures 1–6 on the next page.

The swot

The crammer

Revision techniques

It's one thing to study, but another to actually remember the information. Have you tried these techniques?

a A mnemonic is a way of remembering a list of items by finding a word which contains the first letter of each. For example, to remember the names of the five Great Lakes of America – Huron, Ontario, Erie, Michigan and Superior – take the first letter of each and re-order them to make the word HOMES. Now every time you need to remember the names of the lakes, just think of lots of homes by a lake!

b Why not make up tapes of things you have to remember and listen to them on the way home from school, when you're cleaning your teeth, or even when you're sleeping.

c Little rhymes and chants help you to remember all sorts of information. For instance, if you want to remember the spelling of the word *beautiful*, you can learn this chant:

Mr B, Mr E, Mr A-U-T, Mr I, Mr F-U-L!

d Make up some question and answer cards, and play a quiz game with your friends. Add new questions every time you play it.

e Try putting your different revision notes on different coloured paper.

f Bombardment is a way of constantly reminding yourself of facts. Draw huge multi-coloured fact charts and posters for Science, History, Geography, and any other subject where there are a lot of facts to learn. Stick them everywhere – inside your bedroom door, on your wardrobe, in the kitchen.

6 If you were revising for an English exam, which technique(s) would you use to remember:

  a groups of words?
  b irregular verb forms?
  c pronunciation?
  d tenses?

7 Discuss how useful these techniques are. Talk about any other revision techniques you know.

8 Write your own magazine feature called *Revision Techniques*. Choose the techniques you find most useful, and include your own examples.

Think about it!

1 **How do people feel and behave when they are under stress? Write three more sentences.**

   They bite their nails.

   ....

   ....

   ....

2 **Now write three more ways for people to deal with stress.**

   They should get plenty of sleep.

   ....

   ....

   ....

3 **Write sentences in the second conditional about these people.**

   (a) tired / get more exercise
        If he got more exercise,
        he wouldn't feel tired.

   (b) not organized / make a revision timetable
        ....
        ....

   (c) can't sleep / not drink coffee
        ....
        ....

   Choose and circle.

   Easy   OK   Difficult

Revision

Stop and think!

- Do the exercises on pages 72–75. Start with section A, 'Describing feelings'.
- Look at the HELP screens if you need more practice.

A	Describing feelings	OK	HELP
B	Present perfect/ past simple	OK	HELP
C	Present perfect questions	OK	HELP
D	*used to*	OK	HELP
E	Second conditional	OK	HELP

- Colour each letter when you can do the section.

(A) (B) (C) (D) (E)

Well done!

A
- Look at the Glossary on page 52.
- Do Workbook Unit 11 Exercises 1–2.
- Read item 9 of the Grammar Summary.

B
- Look at the Focus boxes on pages 57 and 61.
- Do Workbook Unit 12 Exercise 8 and Workbook Unit 13 Exercise 9.
- Read item 10 of the Grammar Summary.

C
- Look at the Focus box on page 61.
- Do Workbook Unit 13 Exercises 7–8.
- Read item 10 of the Grammar Summary.

D
- Look at the Focus box on page 65.
- Do Workbook Unit 14 Exercises 4–5.
- Read item 11 of the Grammar Summary.

E
- Look at the Focus box on page 69.
- Do Workbook Unit 15 Exercises 3–4.
- Read item 12 of the Grammar Summary.

A Describing feelings

1 Complete the sentences with one of the adjectives below.

confident   afraid   embarrassed   jealous
moody   optimistic   pessimistic   shy

1 Jenny sleeps with the light on because she is .... of the dark.

2 A person who changes quickly from being happy to being unhappy for no reason is ....

3 Timmy always thinks everything will be all right in the end; he is very ....

4 Sammy always thinks that everything is going to go wrong; he is very ....

5 I was .... when I told a joke in front of the whole class and nobody laughed.

6 .... people feel good about themselves and are not afraid to speak to others.

7 Tommy felt very .... when he saw his girlfriend speak to another boy.

8 Betty finds it very hard to make friends because she is so ....

● B Present perfect/past simple

1 Put the verbs in brackets into the present perfect or the past simple.

- Do you want to see this film?
- I _'ve seen_ (see) it. I _went_ (go) with Sue last week.

1

- Where is your homework?
- I'm sorry, I .... (not/do) it. I .... (have to) visit my aunt last night.

2

- Where is my chicken sandwich?
- I think the dog .... (eat) it. I .... (hear) him eating something a minute ago.

3

- Let's go on that!
- I .... (be) on it already. It .... (make) me sick.

4

- Where are all the children?
- They .... (go) home. I .... (tell) them I didn't want to see them again.

5

- I think the cat's hungry.
- Yes, I .... (not/feed) him yet. I .... (forget) to buy his food this morning.

2 Write four things that you have done, or experiences you have had. Say when you did/had them.

I've been to Paris. I went there in 1997.

● C Present perfect questions

1 Complete the table with the past simple form and past participle of the verbs.

Base Form	Past	Past Participle
buy	bought	bought
do	did	done
drink	....	....
eat	....	....
forget	....	....
have	....	....
make	....	....
meet	....	....
ride	....	....
see	....	....
sleep	....	....

2 Write questions in the present perfect. Use _Have you ever...?_ Then write true answers.

(visit/Japan?) ..._- Have you ever visited Japan?_....
..._- No, I haven't._.................

1 (eat/snake?) _Have_ ....
.... ?
....

2 (meet/famous person?)........................
.... ?
....

3 (have/nightmare?) ....
.... ?
....

4 (ride/horse?).......................................
.... ?
....

5 (fail/exam?) ....
.... ?
....

6 (drink/too much coffee?) ....
.... ?
....

7 (forget/your name?) ....
.... ?
....

8 (sleep/in a tent?)................................
.... ?
....

D *used to*

1 Mrs Godfrey was once very rich, but she lost all of her money last year. Compare her life now to what it used to be like a year ago.

Last year	Today
I was very rich	I haven't got much money
I lived in a very big house	I live in a tiny flat
I drove a Rolls Royce	I haven't got a car
I ate in restaurants every day	I never eat in restaurants
I went on holiday three time a year	I can't afford to go on holidays
I was invited to lots of big parties	I'm never invited to parties
I knew lots of famous people	My old friends don't talk to me

She used to be very rich but now *she hasn't got much money.*

2 Write sentences with *used to* and the words in brackets.

Tom works in an office. He <u>used to work in a</u> <u>factory</u>. (factory)

1 John and Mary live in London. They .... (Manchester)

2 I don't like playing football any more. .... (love it)

3 This club is really boring now. .... (exciting)

4 We hardly ever go to the cinema these days. .... (every week)

E Second conditional

1 Match and join the two parts of the sentences using *would* or *wouldn't*.

If you went to bed earlier, you	.... shout at us.
If Helen studied harder, she	.... have to walk to school.
If I had more money, I	.... get bored and lonely.
If you didn't have a bicycle, you	.... pass all her exams.
If they took more exercise, they	.... be able to buy a car.
If we all failed our test, our teacher	.... be so unfit.
If I stayed in every evening, I	<u>wouldn't</u> be so tired.

2 Look at the pictures. In your notebook, rewrite the sentences using the second conditional.

He eats too much chocolate. He's unhealthy.

If he didn't eat too much chocolate, he wouldn't be unhealthy.

1 I don't like horror movies. I won't go with you.

2 The boots are too small. He won't buy them.

3 The car isn't big enough. They won't all fit in.

4 Trudy is very busy. She won't answer the door.

3 Complete the sentences in your own words.

If I saw a ghost, ...

If I found $1000 in the street, ...

If I met my favourite film star, ...

If I could live anywhere in the world, ...

● Reading and writing

1 Read about Sam Price's dream.

Sam Price was watching TV at home with his wife. It was a film about the life of Elvis Presley. It was a good film, and Sam was a big Elvis Presley fan, but he was very tired. After a while, his eyes closed and he fell into a deep sleep.

He dreamt he was in Memphis, Tennessee, in the 1960s. He was visiting Graceland, the home of Elvis Presley. He was standing in a large, cool room with white walls, and on the table in front of him, there was a gold ring. He picked it up and read the initials 'EP'. At that moment, he began to hear music in the next room, so he went to see who was there. It was Elvis himself,

together with some friends, and they were all laughing and singing and playing guitars.

Sam listened for a while, and when they finished the song, he started clapping. Elvis looked up and noticed Sam for the first time. 'Sam,' he said. 'Sam!' Suddenly, Sam woke up. His wife, Emily, was calling his name. 'Sam, turn the TV off, the film's over.' Sam rubbed his eyes and yawned. 'I was having a strange dream,' he said. 'It was so real.'

His wife went upstairs, but Sam stayed in his chair. He was looking at a gold ring on the table next to him. 'That's funny,' he thought. 'Where did this come from?' He picked up the ring and read the initials, 'EP'.

2 Answer the questions.

1 What was Sam Price doing when he fell asleep?

....

2 Why do you think he dreamt about Elvis Presley?

....

3 Why did his wife wake him up?

....

4 Where do you think the ring came from? Discuss it with your friend.

....

3 Write about a dream you have had. Talk about:

● where you were
● how you felt
● what happened

● Project idea

Keeping a Dream Diary

● Keep a notebook and pencil by your bed.

● As soon as you wake up, write down everything you remember about your dreams.

● After a month, bring your Dream Diary into class and see if you can interpret your dreams.

1 Look at the photos from different films. How many of the films can you name?

2 Which is your favourite film? Tell your partner why you like it.

3 Look at the film posters on the opposite page. Have you seen either of these films? Which film would you like to go and see?

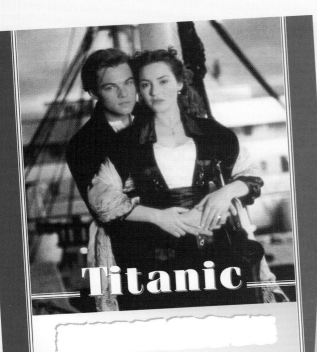

Titanic

This film is very exciting and dramatic but it is also romantic, and very sad. It is about the ship the Titanic which sank in the Atlantic in 1912. The plot is a simple love story. It stars Leonardo Di Caprio and Kate Winslett. They fall in love aboard the ship, but are not allowed to be together as she is rich and he is poor. He is excellent as poor, handsome Jack and Kate Winslett is perfect as rich and beautiful Rose. The best thing about the film is the part where the ship is sinking. It is very realistic and exciting but also very sad. This love story doesn't have a happy ending.

Flubber

Flubber is a comedy starring Robin Williams as a forgetful scientist. He is so forgetful he even forgets his own wedding! Flubber is the name of the amazing green stuff that he invents. The plot is about two bad guys who try to steal both Flubber and Robin Williams's girlfriend. Robin Williams has lots of silly adventures with Flubber, and he is really funny as the mad scientist. The best thing about the film is the special effects as Flubber changes into all different shapes and sizes and even does a dance routine. It's a really enjoyable film.

4 Read the film reviews and complete the texts with the correct caption.

> Forbidden Love On Doomed Ship

> A Comedy For All The Family

5 Read the reviews again and complete the table with information about the films.

name of film	type of film	stars	best thing about film
Titanic	love story		
Flubber		Robin Williams	special effects

6 Think of a film that you have seen or know about and add information about it to the table.

7 In groups, make illustrated film review posters about films you have seen. Draw pictures and write a short text like the ones you have just read.

8 Display the film posters on the classroom wall. Have a class vote to see which is the best one.

Game shows

1   Look at the photos of TV game shows. Do you like watching TV game shows? Why/why not? Does anyone in your family like watching them?

2   In pairs, make a list of all the TV game shows you can think of.

Hold On Tight!

team A ▽

team B ▶

O M E B
F G N
L D I P S
R T A C

3 Look at the photos above. Would you like to be on this game show?

4 Read the text about the game show. What is the prize for the winner?

Gladiators is an American game show which is now very popular in Britain. Individual players fight against a team of very strong Gladiators. The men and women who take part have to be very fit and strong too. Some of the games are quite dangerous, and sometimes people get hurt, but it is very exciting. At the end, the two competitors have a race. The person who wins the race goes on to the next show. The prize at the end of the series is usually a sports car or a motorcycle. The winner really deserves it!

5 Play the Hold On Tight! game. Divide your group into two teams. Each team writes a question card for each hexagon like the ones below.

▶ What 'C' is the fastest animal in the world?
(the cheetah)

▶ What 'R' is the capital of Italy?
(Rome)

6 The two teams take it in turns to answer the questions and cross the board. The first team to get to the other side is the winner.

		love	like	hate
Meat and Fish	chicken			
	beef			
	lamb			
	tuna			
	....			
	....			
Vegetables	potatoes			
	....			
	....			
	....			
	....			
Fruit	apples			
	oranges			
	....			
	....			

1 In pairs, look at the photos and say which types of foods you like and don't like.

2 Do a food preference survey like the one above. Add foods from your country to the list. Ask your partner which of the foods on your list they love, like or hate.

Cafe Picasso

Starter
soup of the day
seafood salad

Main Course
steak and chips
salmon with new potatoes

Dessert
chocolate cake with
raspberry sauce
ice cream

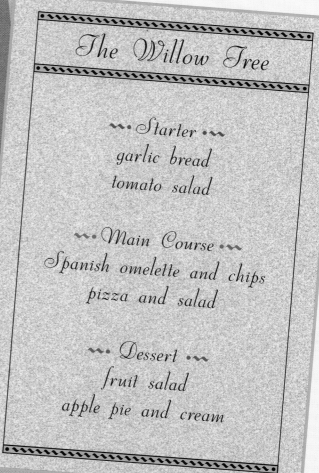

The Willow Tree

···Starter···
garlic bread
tomato salad

···Main Course···
Spanish omelette and chips
pizza and salad

···Dessert···
fruit salad
apple pie and cream

---

3 Compare your survey with the rest of the class. Which is the most popular meat, fish, vegetable and fruit? Which is the most unpopular?

4 Read the two menus above. Which menu do you prefer? Why?

5 Work in pairs to create a menu. Include different choices for the starter, main course and dessert. Think of a name for your cafe and illustrate your menu with pictures.

6 Display your menus on the classroom wall. Which cafe would you like to visit most?

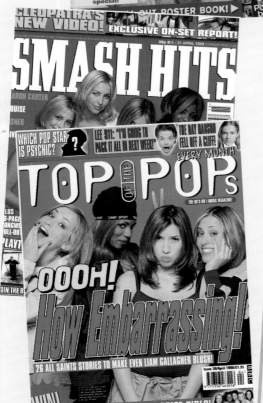

HOT! Star Questionnaire

We asked Danny from the band 777 a few questions. Here are his answers.

What is the best thing about being famous?

Danny Well, there's the money of course. But the best thing must be all the nice letters and photos that my fans send me - especially the girl fans!

What's the worst thing about being famous?

Danny I guess the hardest thing is when the newspapers tell stupid lies about you.

What is the first thing you think about when you wake up?

Danny Breakfast!

What do you want to do next when you have finished your world tour?

Danny Nothing! I'm tired out and need a holiday!

---

1 Look at these magazines. What sort of things are inside them?

2 Do you read magazines like this? What do you like about them?

3 Read the HOT! magazine Star Questionnaire. What does Danny want to do next?

Dear Robbie and Mel ...

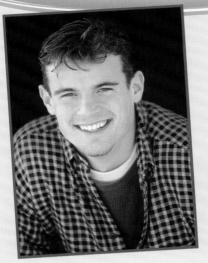

**Share your worries with Robbie and Mel
on the (HOT!) Letters Page.
They'll answer your problems, big or small.**

Nice Legs!

I'm a boy and I help in a sports shop on Saturdays. The problem is I have to wear shorts. All the girls in the shop talk about me and laugh. I play a lot of football and my mum says I've got nice legs, but I'm really embarrassed. The girls who work in the shop sometimes wear trousers but I'm not allowed. What can I do?

Leave me alone, Mum!

I'm hardly ever allowed to go out with my friends. When I do, my mum always gives me a long talk about taking care and being sensible. I know all this already and I am always really careful and sensible. How can I make her trust me?

---

4 Read the HOT! letters page. In pairs, write answers to the letters.

5 In groups, produce your own magazine. Each pair in your group should work on a different part of the magazine. Your magazine should have a letters page, a pop star questionnaire, film and TV reviews, and a puzzle and jokes page. When you have finished, put all the different bits of the magazine together. Think of a name for your magazine and design a front cover.

6 Present your magazine to the class. Have a class vote to see which is the best one.

Grammar Summary

1 past simple: irregular verbs

A lot of verbs have an irregular form in the past simple. There are no rules for the formation of irregular past verb forms. The past forms of *go* and *have*, for example are *went* and *had*.

They went to India last week.
They had an interesting holiday.

2 past simple: *be*

a statements

The verb *be* has an irregular past form. The singular form is *was / wasn't* and the plural is *were / weren't*.

She wasn't very good at Maths, but she was good at sports.
They were at primary school together, but they weren't at secondary school together.

b questions

What were your favourite subjects?
  My favourite subjects were …
Who was your best friend?
  My best friend was …

Were you happy at school?
  No, I wasn't.
Was your favourite subject English?
  Yes, it was.

3 adverbs

a adverbs of frequency

We can use adverbs of frequency to talk about habits or repeated actions.

never   sometimes   often   usually   always
0%   100%

We often use them with the present simple. They usually come

● after the verb *be*

  He's never on time.
  They're often in the office.

● before other verbs

  They sometimes play tennis.
  She always wears a uniform.

b adverbs of manner

We can use adverbs of manner to give extra information about an action or feeling. To make these adverbs we add *-ly* to adjectives.

Amanda picked up the phone nervously.
You need to speak more clearly.
She always does her homework carefully.

4 need to / have to / don't have to

We can use these modal verbs to talk about what is and is not necessary. They are always followed by an infinitive. Need to and have to are very similar in meaning.

You have to sing a song.
You need to have a bike.
You don't have to be a great musician.
You needn't be a great artist.

5 past simple

a use

We can use the past simple tense to talk about actions and events in the past.

I collected a lot of money.
I didn't have time to talk to Eddie.

b spelling of regular past forms

Use this table to help you.

verb	spelling	regular past form
collect	+ -ed	collected
talk		talked
hate	+ -d	hated
damage		damaged
drop	double letter + -ed	dropped
bury	y → ied	buried
study		studied

c   irregular verbs

Here are a few irregular verbs you have seen in this book.

verb	irregular past form
become	became
begin	began
feel	felt
forget	forgot
make	made
put	put
teach	taught
write	wrote

6   present passive

a   use and form

One use of the present passive is to describe the stages of a process.

The magazine is designed on a computer.

We make the present passive like this:

subject + *am/is/are* + past participle

The text   is   checked.

b   *by*

We use *by* with the passive when we want to say who or what does the action.

The photos are chosen by the designer.

7   past continuous

We can use the past continuous to describe an action in the past which is interrupted.

The girl was picking grapes when Vesuvius errupted.
What were you doing when the earthquake started?
Were you watching TV?
I wasn't watching TV, I was cooking dinner.

The past continuous is formed like this:

subject + the past of *be* + the *-ing* form of the verb

The man was mending a wheel when Vesuvius erupted.

8   *should / shouldn't*

We can use *should* and *shouldn't* to talk about what we think is the right or wrong thing to do.

People should take care of the environment.
You shouldn't throw away glass bottles.

9   advice

a   *If I were you ...*

We can give advice by using *If I were you + I would/wouldn't ...*

If I were you, I'd talk to your friend.
If I were you, I wouldn't worry about it.

b   other ways of giving advice

I think you should try harder.
I don't think you should play with that spider.
How about looking in a dictionary?
Why don't you phone the hospital?

10   present perfect simple

a   achievements

We can use the present perfect simple to talk about experiences and achievements. We make the present perfect simple like this:

have/has + past participle

Marcus has been to China.
I haven't been to Australia.
Has he had a hit record?

b   recent events or actions

We can also use the present perfect to talk about very recent events or actions – especially when we can still see the results. We often use *just* to show this.

The boy has just crossed the road.
The red car has just crashed.

c   present perfect and past simple

We can use the present perfect to ask and answer about experiences some time in the past.

Have you ever had a nightmare?

We can use the past simple to talk about a particular experience.

I had a nightmare last night.
Was it frightening?
Yes, it was!

11   used to

We use *used to* to talk about things that we did in the past but don't do any more.

I used to play football every Saturday.
Did you use to work in France?
I didn't use to believe in ghosts.

12 the second conditional

We can use the second conditional to talk about what would happen in imaginary situations. The second conditional is formed like this:

If + past (imaginary situation), ... *would* + base form (what would happen).

If she wasn't so rude, people would like her more.

We can also reverse the clauses in the sentence.

People would like her more if she wasn't so rude.

OXFORD
UNIVERSITY PRESS

Great Clarendon Street, Oxford OX2 6DP

Oxford University Press is a department of the University of Oxford.
It furthers the University's objective of excellence in research, scholarship,
and education by publishing worldwide in

Oxford New York

Auckland Cape Town Dar es Salaam Hong Kong Karachi
Kuala Lumpur Madrid Melbourne Mexico City Nairobi
New Delhi Shanghai Taipei Toronto

With offices in

Argentina Austria Brazil Chile Czech Republic France Greece
Guatemala Hungary Italy Japan Poland Portugal Singapore
South Korea Switzerland Thailand Turkey Ukraine Vietnam

OXFORD and OXFORD ENGLISH are registered trade marks of
Oxford University Press in the UK and in certain other countries

ISBN: 978 0 19 435904 7

Printed in China

ACKNOWLEDGEMENTS

*The authors and publisher are grateful to those who have given permission to reproduce
the following extracts and adaptations of copyright material*:

p 33 With kind permission of Comic Relief.

p 46 'Human Garbage Disposal Eats Trash!' by permission of Weekly World
News.

p 63 Extract from Childlines by permission of Ringpress Books Ltd, P.O. Box
8, Lydney, Gloucestershire GL15 6YD.

Illustrations by: Kathy Baxendale pp 30, 31 (letter), 54, 55 (letter); Jenny
Brackley pp 31 (hobbies), 63; Brett Breckon pp 39, 62; Chris Brown pp 6, 14,
15 (house), 26, 40, 48, 60, 69 (relieving exam stress), 75; Michael Brownlow
pp 5 (Sparks), 9 (Sparks), 13 (Sparks), 17 (Sparks), 21 (Sparks), 29, 37 (Sparks),
38 (Sparks), 41 (Sparks), 45 (Sparks), 53, 57, 61, 65 (Sparks), 69 (Sparks); Sally
Chambers pp 25 (groceries), 38 (dice, spinner, paper, counters), 44, 47 (bottle,
chest, hat, knife); Kevin Faerbar p 7 (teenagers); Christyan Fox/Beint & Beint
pp 19, 43; Neil Gower pp 22, 41 (Herculaneum); Lorraine Harrison pp 28
(logos), 67 (background); Barbara Lofthouse/Artist Partners p 42; Lisa
McCormick pp 29 (chart), 47 (poster); Michael Ogden pp 8, 11; Bill Piggins
pp 25, 55 (girls, boys), 65 (man in suit, man in casual clothes), 71 (boy looking
tired, disorganized student, insomniac boy), 73, 74 (girl seeing a ghost, boy in
street, girl meeting a film star, boy on island); Mark Ruffle p 36; Francis
Scappaticci/Mundy Illustration p 71 (remembering information); Tim Slade
pp 7 (animals), 37 (flow charts), 56, 67 (activities); Bart Verney pp 23, 28 (ice-
skater, dancer, gymnast), 42, 45 (kind to the environment), 50, 68, 69 (girl
chewing, boy eating chocolate, girl worrying, boy with books, boy drinking
coffee), 70, 74 (unhealthy man, boy and girl, man trying on boots, Mini, girl
doing revision)

Model by: Tim Ruffle pp 36, 38

Commissioned photography by: Julie Fisher

*The publisher would like to thank the following organizations for their help and co-
operation*: Channel 4 News; St. James' Catholic School, Colindale; Radio
Oxygen, Oxford; Mr. Young's Preview Theatre, London

*The publisher would like to thank the following for their permission to reproduce
photographs*: Anthony Blake Photo Library p 80 (pizza, ice cream, carrots,
chocolate cake)/Gerrit Buntrock p 80 (salad, spaghetti)/Tim Hill p 80 (steak)/
Maximilian p 80 (milk, rice, chips)/Rosenfeld p 80 (egg, bananas)/Andrew
Sydenham p 80 (tomato soup); Aquarius Library p 76 (Spiceworld, Star Wars)/
Lucas Film Ltd/Paramount p 76 (Indiana Jones)/20th Century Fox p 77
(Titanic); BBC Television p 78 (Shooting Stars); John Birdsall pp 64 (cycling,
weights); Carlton Television p 78 (Family Fortunes); J. Allan Cash pp 6 (camel),
18 (The Globe), 64 (climbing); Corbis Everett p 76 (Anastasia), (Tomorrow
Never Dies)/Warner Brothers TMS and © 1997 DC Comics p 76 (Batman and
Robin); Bruce Coleman p 6 (cheetah, tiger, butterfly, kiwi); Sylvia Cordaiy pp 6
(chihuahua), 16 (Shakespeare), 17 (ampitheatre), 28 (badges); Ecoscene p 44
(bottlebank); Fortean Picture Library p 59; Getty Images p 82; James Darrell
p 83 (Mel); Sally & Richard Greenhill p 28 (football); Hutchison Photo Library
p 18 (Noh Theatre); Image bank p 66; Nicolas Ryssell p 83 (Robbie); Kobal
Collection/ Amblin/Universal p 76 (Jurassic Park); © Disney Enterprises p 77
(Flubber); London Weekend Television p 78 (Ice Warriors), (Blind Date), p 79
(Strike it Rich); Performing Arts Library p 16 (ballet); Pictures p 80 (fish,
hamburger); Redferns p 16 (rock group); Rex Features pp 43 (earthquake), 63;
Scottish Television p 78 (Wheel of Fortune); Still Pictures p 6 (blue whale,
dolphin, shark); Stockshot p 64 (snowboarding); Tony Stone Wordwide pp 6
(tortoise), 13 (skydivers), 40, 44 (cycling), 64 (swimming); Trip/Helene Rogers
p 28 (jewellery, coins, stamps, dolls); John Walmsley pp 28 (chess), 51
(football, snooker, horseriding), 64 (windsurfing, martial arts, yoga); Janine
Wiedel Photography pp 28 (making things), 51 (chess); World Pictures p 41

The publisher would like to thank the following for their kind permission to
reproduce the front covers: Big, Smash Hits, TV Hits, Top of the Pops.

Cover illustration by: Michael Brownlow